The Practitioner's Bookshelf

Hands-On Literacy Books for
Classroom Teachers and Administrators

Dorothy S. Strickland
FOUNDING EDITOR, LANGUAGE AND LITERACY SERIES

Celia Genishi and Donna E. Alvermann
LANGUAGE AND LITERACY SERIES EDITORS*

Academic Literacy for English Learners:
High-Quality Instruction Across Content Areas
Cynthia Brock, Diane Lapp, Rachel Salas, and Dianna Townsend

Literacy for Real:
Reading, Thinking, and Learning in the Content Areas
ReLeah Cossett Lent

Teaching Individual Words:
One Size Does Not Fit All
Michael F. Graves

Literacy Essentials for English Language Learners:
Successful Transitions
Maria Uribe and Sally Nathenson-Mejía

Literacy Leadership in Early Childhood:
The Essential Guide
Dorothy S. Strickland and Shannon Riley-Ayers

* For a list of current titles in the Language and Literacy Series, see *www.tcpress.com*

Academic Literacy for English Learners

HIGH-QUALITY INSTRUCTION ACROSS CONTENT AREAS

CYNTHIA BROCK

DIANE LAPP

RACHEL SALAS

DIANNA TOWNSEND

Foreword by Douglas Fisher

Teachers College
Columbia University
New York and London

Published by Teachers College Press, 1234 Amsterdam Avenue, New York, NY 10027

Copyright © 2009 by Teachers College, Columbia University

All rights reserved. No part of this publication may be reproduced or transmitted in any form or by any means, electronic or mechanical, including photocopy, or any information storage and retrieval system, without permission from the publisher.

Library of Congress Cataloging-in-Publication Data

Academic literacy for English learners : high-quality instruction across
    content areas / Cynthia Brock ... [et al.] ; foreword by Douglas
    Fisher.
      p. cm. — (The practitioner's bookshelf)
  Includes bibliographical references and index.
  ISBN 978-0-8077-5009-4 (pbk. : alk. paper)
    1. English language—Study and teaching—Foreign speakers.
2. Language arts—Correlation with content subjects—United States.
3. Second language acquisition. 4. Linguistic minorities—Education—
Social aspects. 5. Language and culture. I. Brock, Cynthia H.
  PE1128.A2.A212 2009
  428.2'4—dc22   2009015340

ISBN 978-0-8077-5009-4 (paper)

Printed on acid-free paper
Manufactured in the United States of America

16 15 14 13 12 11 10 09   8 7 6 5 4 3 2 1

Contents

Foreword:
Calming the Sea by Conversing

IN 1983, JAMES BRITTON SUGGESTED that "Reading and writing float on a sea of talk" (p. 29). One can infer that he meant that the ability of humans to engage in sophisticated literacy practices, like making meaning from print, was built on a foundation of speech. Parents and teachers alike know that speech develops earlier than reading and writing, and so on some level Britton's comment resonates with us all.

But I think that his comment was more profound than that. I think that Britton was onto something very important, and often neglected in discussions of literacy instruction, especially for English learners. If we are to develop academic literacy—the literacy of higher education and the workplace—we must attend to students' oral language development. And it's more than just simply getting students to talk. Any substitute teacher knows that students will talk on their own. It's the *type of talk* that moves students to *proficient* levels of reading and writing.

Interestingly, Britton chose the word *sea* in his metaphor. When I think of the sea, I think of wide expanses, deepness, and a certain amount of danger (à la *The Perfect Storm*). And for decades, teachers have attempted to calm that sea in their classrooms and facilitate student interactions—talk—so that students become proficient in the language of instruction.

And this book does just that. It provides teachers with very specific information about instructional routines useful in facilitating student-to-student interaction. It moves beyond simple "engagement" activities to purposeful conversations that leave the participants better for the experience. This book also provides readers

with glimpses into classrooms in which teachers guide and facilitate student talk. In other words, it charts a new course in teaching
and learning, providing maps along the way.

Calming the sea is not easy, but it is important. In fact, it is the
only way that English learners will develop academic proficiency.
Simply forcing them to engage in isolated skills instruction hasn't
worked; they need to talk with their peers and teachers in meaningful ways, and this book explicates how to accomplish this. Yes, this
book calms the sea by creating classrooms in which conversations
occur.

—Douglas Fisher

Preface

ARE YOU WONDERING ABOUT HOW to teach the English learners in your classroom? If so, you are not alone. This question is one we have pondered among ourselves. As a result, we highlight instructional practices that support the learning of English learners in this book. While literacy serves as the underlying foundation of the entire book, a unique feature of the text is that it was designed and written by educators with disciplinary expertise, including literacy, academic English, English as a Second Language, mathematics, social studies, and science. The common thread among this interdisciplinary group of educators is a commitment to designing effective and meaningful instruction for English learners, with the explicit goal of fostering high levels of academic English proficiency.

The first chapter of the book describes the social, cultural, and linguistic backgrounds of English learners in American schools. Chapters 2–4 provide windows into public school classrooms with first-, third-, and fifth-grade teachers who serve students from a wide variety of academic, cultural, linguistic, and socioeconomic backgrounds. The four authors of this book worked closely with content specialists so that the chapters authentically and meaningfully integrate literacy and various content areas—specifically, science in Grade 1 (Chapter 2), mathematics in Grade 3 (Chapter 3), and social studies in Grade 5 (Chapter 4)—with special emphasis on fostering high levels of academic English proficiency for English learners. The final chapter provides explicit information that we hope will help you to design integrated lessons similar to those we've shared in this book. As a further guide, the lesson models employed in Chapters 2–4 are summarized in the Appendices.

We use several conventions throughout this text that we wish to share with you as a reader. All of the authors of this text have been public school teachers or currently are teaching in public schools. Additionally, all of us have worked closely with public school teachers. The teachers we highlight in this text are composite portraits of the many teachers we have worked with across the years. The same holds true for the students we discuss. All of the authors have taught many English learners. Additionally, we have worked with English learners in other teachers' classrooms. Thus, the English learners we highlight in this text are composite portraits of the many students we have worked with across the years. Finally, many labels (e.g., second language learners, English language learners, language minority students) have been used in the literature to refer to children who do not speak English as a first language (August & Shanahan, 2006). While no labels are perfect, and likely have some drawbacks, we use the term *English learners* (ELs) throughout this text to refer to students who do not speak English as a first language and who are learning English as an additional language.

Acknowledgments

W E WISH TO ACKNOWLEDGE our friend and colleague, Dr. Jim Flood, for sharing his insightful thoughts and ideas about the topics we address in this book during its initial planning stages. We are deeply indebted to our friend and colleague, Dr. Douglas Fisher, Professor of Education, San Diego State University, for writing the Foreword to our book. Special thanks to the following people for the pictures we use throughout the text: Dr. Linda Lungren and Joe Russo; the teachers and students at E. B. Scripps Elementary School in San Diego, California; and the teachers and students at Glenn Duncan Elementary School in Reno, Nevada. Finally, we sincerely thank Meg Lemke and Susan Liddicoat from Teachers College Press for their thoughtful and careful editing and guidance throughout the process of writing this book.

Academic Literacy for English Learners

HIGH-QUALITY INSTRUCTION ACROSS CONTENT AREAS

CHAPTER 1

Instruction That Supports English Learners

Cynthia Brock, Rachel Salas,
Diane Lapp, and Dianna Townsend

AS THERESA MILLER OBSERVED the children in her first-grade classroom, who were engaged in partner talk about the decision being faced by the family presented in Eve Bunting's *Sunshine Home* (2005), she reaffirmed her belief regarding the importance of purposeful conversation as a practice in learning, developing, and becoming comfortable with one's second language. Moving among the partner teams, Ms. Miller supported the children's predictions about whether the family would bring Grandmother home. Following a minute or two of whole-group sharing of their predictions, she continued the read-aloud of this story about the difficult and complex decisions faced by a family when an elderly family member is placed in a nursing home. She chose this book because it contained experiences that were very familiar to her students. She knew this would support the children's conversation and writing as they made text-to-self comparisons.

One of Ms. Miller's major concerns is how to provide effective instruction for her students who are learning English in a classroom with fluent English speakers (Rockoff, 2004). She understands their stresses, since she is learning Spanish as a second language.

Like almost 90% of the teachers in American public schools, Ms. Miller is a European American, monolingual woman (National Center for Educational Statistics, 2000). She and many other monolingual teachers are teaching increasingly more English learners in their classrooms (National Center for Educational Statistics, 2002). For example, Thomas and Collier (2001) estimate that by the year 2040, children who speak a first language other than English will make up 40% of the children in American public schools. Currently, in California, where Ms. Miller teaches, English is not the first language for well over half of the children in public schools (Garcia & Montavon, 2007). The demographics in Ms. Miller's classroom reflect several other national trends. The majority of English learners in Ms. Miller's classroom speak Spanish as a first language, while other ELs speak Asian languages as their first languages. Nationally, almost half of the immigrants who came to the United States in the 1990s were from Latin American countries, one-fourth came from Asian countries, and the remaining immigrants came from countries all over the world (Malone, Baluja, Constanzo, & Davis, 2003).

Ms. Miller knows that many English learners are, and historically have been, underserved in American public schools (Lewis & Bachman, 2003; Strickland & Alvermann, 2004; Thomas & Collier, 2001). For example, English learners tend to receive lower scores on standardized tests than their native-English-speaking counterparts, and they tend to be over-represented in remedial programs and lower academic tracks in public school systems (Fitzgerald & Graves, 2004; Garcia & Wold, 2006). Why English learners have been underserved in American public schools cannot be answered simply. Nieto (2004) suggests one important answer that we, as an educational community, must confront. We need to "challenge the conventional wisdom concerning the abilities and skills" of ELs entering U.S. classrooms (p. xiii). We must believe that they are knowledgeable people who *do* speak a language and are trying to learn a second language.

As mentioned earlier, almost 90% of the teaching force in American public schools comprises European American, monolingual English-speaking women, who increasingly are teaching English learners whose cultural and linguistic backgrounds are very different from their own. This difference matters for two important reasons. First, while well intentioned, these teachers may not be aware of the rich cultural and linguistic backgrounds of their students (Goldstein, 2004). This lack of knowledge can result in teachers' misunderstanding and underestimating the abilities and skills of ELs and not drawing on their rich and unique cultural and linguistic backgrounds to design classroom lessons (Díaz-Rico & Weed, 2002). Second, even if teachers realize that their English learners bring rich cultural and linguistic backgrounds to their classrooms, they may not know how to craft the most effective classroom lessons to facilitate the learning of these students (Lenski, Ehlers-Zavala, Daniel, & Sun-Irminger, 2006). This book has been designed to offer some possibilities, as we take you inside the classrooms of three teachers to share their attempts to integrate language, literacy, and content curriculum.

INTRODUCING THREE TEACHERS AND THEIR STUDENTS

Ms. Miller's First-Grade Classroom

At the beginning of this chapter, you met Ms. Miller. Her class has 19 first-graders who speak a range of first languages, including English, Spanish, Somali, Korean, Cantonese, Vietnamese, Black English, and Arabic. In Chapter 2 we focus on three of the children in this classroom: Susana, Asad, and James. Susana is a five-year-old child who immigrated to the United States from Mexico when she was three. Asad was born in the United States to parents who had come here from Somalia three years earlier. James was born in a rural community in Georgia and speaks Black English Vernacular.

Mrs. Wood's Third-Grade Classroom

Mrs. Wood is a third-grade European American teacher in a small community located near Portland, Oregon. Her school has an ESL teacher; however, Mrs. Wood's district does not have any bilingual education programs. A teacher for eight years, Mrs. Wood has a longstanding interest in mathematics as well as literacy. Both her undergraduate and graduate studies emphasized the meaningful integration of subjects to promote student learning, and she has learned from her own reflective teaching experiences that meaningful thematic teaching promotes the learning of all of her students—especially her English learners. Approximately two-thirds of the 26 children in this classroom are European American and speak English as their first language. The remaining children are Latino and speak Spanish as their first language.

Adriana, Homero, and Gabriela are the three students who will be the focus of Chapter 3. Adriana and her family moved to the Pacific Northwest from Mexico just prior to her entering Mrs. Wood's classroom; she reads and writes Spanish at the beginning third-grade level. Homero was born in the United States, but Spanish is his first language. Mrs. Wood characterizes Homero as the top student academically (in English) in her classroom. Gabriela was born in Guatemala. She and her family moved to the United States when Gabriela was six and one-half years old, and they enrolled her in first grade.

Mrs. Weber's Fifth-Grade Classroom

Mrs. Weber, a fifth-grade teacher in the Midwest, is a European American, monolingual English speaker. She has a bachelor's degree in elementary education, an ESL endorsement, and a master's degree in social studies education. A 20-year veteran full-time teacher, Mrs. Weber currently is enrolled in a Ph.D. program in elementary education.

In Chapter 4 we focus on three children in Mrs. Weber's classroom: Carolina, Elena, and Javier. Carolina, a native of Guatemala, has been in the United States for six months. She is in the initial stages of learning English. Elena's mother came to the United States from El Salvador 12 years ago. Elena was born in the United States and Spanish is her first language. Elena can speak, read, and write in English, and she is in the process of developing academic English skills. Javier is fluent in Spanish and English. Both of Javier's parents have advanced college degrees, and Spanish and English are spoken, written, and read in his home. Javier is fluent in conversational and academic English for his age and grade level.

Learning to provide effective instruction for all English learners involves knowing about the second language acquisition process as well as understanding how interactions can vary across cultural contexts. In the following two sections, we discuss both of these issues. As you read, we invite you to think about the English learners you teach as well as those whom you are meeting in this text. Ask yourself how the ideas we present about second language acquisition and cross-cultural interactions may relate to all of these children who are in the process of learning English as an additional language.

THE COMPLEXITIES INVOLVED IN ACQUIRING AN ADDITIONAL LANGUAGE

If you have ever tried to learn an additional language to the point of attaining native-like proficiency, you undoubtedly have some idea about the arduous process involved in second language acquisition (Echevarria, Vogt, & Short, 2004; Thomas & Collier, 2001). However, consider this: Many ELs in U.S. schools, like Adriana in Mrs. Wood's class, were uprooted from familiar home and cultural surroundings and placed into American school contexts where they did not understand the culture, and couldn't speak, read, or write in the language of instruction. The process of entering U.S. public schools for non-English speakers can be traumatic (Gitlin, Buendia, Crossland, & Doumbia, 2003).

Notwithstanding the trauma that ELs can experience when entering U.S. public schools, the process of learning a new language and culture is long and complex. It takes a minimum of five to seven years for most children to become proficient in a second language (Thomas & Collier, 2001). Consider the many factors that contribute to the second language acquisition process (Cummins, 2001; Freeman & Freeman, 2003). For example, the literacy proficiencies and academic competence a child has acquired in her first language will transfer to her second language (August & Shanahan, 2006). Consequently, the more a child knows and understands about reading and writing processes and purposes in her first language, the less she will have to learn about the purposes and processes of reading and writing in English. Hence, the less time it will take for her to learn to read and write in English. As an example, consider the situation of Gabriela, a student in Mrs. Wood's class. Gabriela had attained oral proficiency in her home language of Spanish. However, because she had just entered first grade in Guatemala prior to moving to the United States with her family, she had very little knowledge about reading and writing in any language. Thus, Gabriela had little background knowledge about the process and purposes of reading and writing to draw on while she was in the process of learning to read and write in English.

Other factors besides reading and writing proficiency in a child's home language impact the second language acquisition process. For example, a child's desire and motivation to learn the second language, the nature of interactions in classrooms to which English learners are assigned, the relationship between the language learner and the classroom teacher, and teacher attitude and expectations all contribute to the time and complexity of acquiring a second language (Brisk, 2002; Burns, 2003).

Unfortunately, well-intentioned teachers inadvertently may sabotage the learning of English learners. One way that this can happen is when teachers misjudge English learners' proficiency levels. Cummins (2001) makes an important and useful distinction between *conversational* and *academic competence* in second language acquisition. Conversational competence involves the ability to use the new language to engage in informal conversations, such as greeting others and talking about the weather. The ability to converse informally, however, is very different from the kind of academic English competence required to understand science, social studies, and mathematics concepts in a new language. This book focuses on instructional practices to promote the acquisition of academic English by ELs.

Understanding complex academic concepts in a new language takes many years to achieve. If teachers mistake basic conversational ability for effective understanding and use of academic English, they may not provide ELs with the necessary support to understand complex ideas in different academic subjects. Without sustained and adequate support, ELs can fall behind in subject-matter learning while they are in the long process of acquiring academic competence in their new language. Again returning to the case of Gabriela, Mrs. Wood recognized that she was experiencing difficulty in the different academic subjects. Clearly, Gabriela will need additional support from her teacher and peers for many years so that she can learn social studies, science, and mathematics concepts while she is in the process of learning English.

When teachers misjudge the milestones that language learners make in the process of acquiring an additional language, they inadvertently may sabotage the learning of English learners. *Interlanguage* is the term linguists apply to the intermediate language that learners speak while they are in the process of acquiring a more formal version of a target language (Freeman & Freeman, 2003). Language learners draw upon four different types of knowledge in constructing interlanguage, including "knowledge about the second language, competence in their native language, ability to use the functions of language, and their general world knowledge" (Díaz-Rico & Weed, 2002, p. 18). Teachers must be aware that interlanguage is different in form from the language spoken by native speakers of English. For example, an English learner may say, "He asked me that should he go." In this case, the language learner has "overgeneralized the question-word-order rule" (Díaz-Rico & Weed, 2002, p. 31). Thus, while the sentence is syntactically incorrect, the language learner has demonstrated the ability to apply a complex cognitive strategy while she is in the process of trying to learn English.

What should or can we do as teachers to help our ELs while they are in this interlanguage phase? According to Díaz-Rico and Weed (2002), the first thing that teachers should *not* do is to see their ELs as "bumblers whose every mistake needs 'fixing'" (p. 36). Instead, teachers should view their ELs as "intelligent, hypothesis-forming individuals who use the knowledge of their first language and a growing awareness of the second to progress toward native-like second language fluency" (p. 36). Some of the most effective ways to help children progress on the continuum toward more native-like proficiency include modeling appropriate use of English in interactions with ELs and providing lots of opportunities for them to interact with native speakers both in and out of the classroom. Additionally, teachers can work with ELs to target one or two skills or strategies at a time to work on in their speaking and writing. As these skills and strategies are mastered, the student and the teacher can move on to new skills and strategies (Díaz-Rico & Weed, 2002; Freeman & Freeman, 2003). Throughout Chapters 2–4 in this book, we provide specific examples of Ms. Miller, Mrs. Wood, and Mrs. Weber working with ELs in meaningful ways to assist them in the process of acquiring more native-like proficiency in English as well as to develop academic English across subjects.

RECOGNIZING DIFFERENT PATTERNS OF INTERACTIONS ACROSS CULTURES

If you have ever spent time in a context that is very different for you, or if you have spoken, in depth, with someone who has, then you know that different cultural groups have different norms, values, beliefs, behaviors, and ways of acting and interacting (Au, 2005). Because we know our own cultures so well, our cultural norms are often tacit and taken for granted; many of us are not aware of the norms that constitute our cultural ways of being. Often the experience of entering into an unfamiliar culture can make us acutely aware that we don't fit in because we don't know the "rules" or norms for how to behave in that new culture.

Just being aware that American classrooms and schools function according to mainstream, middle-class, European American cultural values can help us to understand that there can be a cultural mismatch between schools and the children they serve (Au, 2005). We briefly discuss the work of Shirley Brice Heath and Luis Moll and his colleagues in order to illustrate the significance of potential mismatches between home and school cultures and what educators might do to mitigate these potential mismatches.

When Literacy Practices at Home and School Differ

Shirley Brice Heath (1991) spent 10 years studying the communities, families, and schools in the Piedmont Carolinas. Roadville and Trackton were two communities that she studied extensively. Here's what she learned about the families in those two working-class communities. The families in Trackton were primarily African American, and the families in Roadville were primarily European American. The families in both communities engaged in literacy-related traditions; however, those traditions varied from one community to the other. Reading materials in the homes of Trackton families included newspapers, advertisements, church materials, school notices, and so forth; however, there were few books besides family bibles, school books, and church-oriented books. Newspaper articles and various sections of the newspaper, for example, were discussed socially, and much writing (e.g., church bulletins) was done socially. Thus, the families engaged in literate traditions that were primarily social and group oriented.

Homes in Roadville tended to have considerably more reading materials than Trackton homes. These materials included children's books, magazines, newspapers, and church brochures. Reading and writing practices in Roadville homes varied from practices in Trackton, however. Parents often read to their children before bedtime, but reading involved little questioning or interpretation on the children's part. In general, children were taught to listen passively when adults read to them. Moreover, aside from reading newspapers and magazines, adults did not engage in many sustained reading practices. Families in Roadville mainly engaged in functional writing such as writing letters to family members, writing checks to pay bills, and so forth.

While families in both Roadville and Trackton used literacy in various different ways in their homes and communities, the uses of literacy in each of these groups did not match closely with the ways literacy was used in middle-class homes or the local schools. For example, middle-class families in the local community had considerably more reading materials available in their homes and engaged in a much wider variety of reading and writing activities on a daily basis. One of these practices included reading bedtime stories daily to their children and discussing and critiquing the stories with the children in the ways that teachers typically discussed stories with children in school (Heath, 1991). This particular literacy practice, as well as others engaged in by middle-class families, matched closely with literacy practices in the local schools. Consequently, when children from middle-class families entered schools, they typically experienced more school success because their literacy-related backgrounds and prior experiences were more closely aligned with school-based literacy practices. A key point here is that families from Roadville or Trackton were not deficient in literacy and language-related practices at home, but that those practices varied from practices in the middle-class community and the local schools. When teachers understand that children may come to their classrooms from community contexts in which literacy and language are used differently from the ways they may be used in schools, teachers can work with children, building on the strengths they bring to school, and helping them to appropriate school-based literacy practices.

Changing the Learning Dynamic Between School and Home

In an effort to bridge school and neighborhood communities, Moll and his colleagues (Moll, 1992; Moll & Gonzalez, 1994) have shifted the focus of the "typical" home–school relationship in their powerful and groundbreaking work in the Southwest. Working with many Latino families, Moll and his teacher colleagues have become respectful learners about children, their families, and the communities served by the local schools. They learned that the families had powerful "funds of knowledge," about such topics as working on automobiles and natural herbal medicines, to share in the school context. These funds of knowledge became the foundation on which the teachers built as they helped the children in their classrooms learn to engage in school literacy learning. In this context, the typical focus—requiring or expecting the children and their families to learn about and adapt to the school norms—shifted. Rather than expecting that a one-way bridge be built by parents to the schools, the teachers in Moll's project saw the value of building a two-way bridge between school and home. That is, the teachers valued learning about the cultures and experiences of the children and their families, while helping them learn about the school culture.

UNDERSTANDING HOW STUDENTS LEARN

A cornerstone of the effectiveness of the three teachers you will get to know in this book is their focus on student learning. These teachers know that their instruction is effective only if it meets the needs of the children in their classroom. Thus, all three teachers base instructional decisions on their knowledge about how students learn.

Drawing on their knowledge of learning theorists such as Piaget and Inhelder (1969) and Vygotsky (1978), Ms. Miller, Mrs. Wood, and Mrs. Weber understand that our capacity to learn, as humans, is influenced by our genetic or biological "hardwiring," our language-based interactions with others in different social contexts, and our cultural and historical backgrounds. While these teachers agree that biological factors are important to consider in discussions of learning, they focus on the social and cultural factors as the areas in which they can have the most direct impact in their work with children.

They believe that learning occurs as a result of effective language-based social interactions with others (Vygotsky, 1978). So, for example, complex conceptual processes such as learning to read, write, and speak develop first through directed interactions with others (i.e., parents and teachers). Over time, and with the appropriate guidance (often referred to as "scaffolding"), children begin to "learn" to assume control over the complex processes of speaking, reading, and writing (Clay, 1991; Vygotsky, 1978). Thus, the gist of what we are saying is that learning does not originate in our individual minds; rather, the origin of our individual learning is effectively scaffolded through social interactions with others (Vygotsky, 1978). So, why does all of this matter? Ms. Miller, Mrs. Wood, and Mrs. Weber understand that the very nature of the interactions they structure in their classrooms determines the opportunities their students have for learning school subjects.

Clearly, we have a profound responsibility to think carefully about how we organize and manage interactions in our classroom contexts. However, another important aspect of a sociocultural perspective on learning is that learning is shaped and influenced by more than just immediate interactions in any one context. Our learning also is shaped and influenced by our individual histories as well as our cultural backgrounds (Vygotsky, 1978). At first glance, this tenet of sociocultural theory may not seem like a "big deal." It turns out that it really is. To illustrate this point, we'll again draw on the example of the work of Shirley Brice Heath (1991), which we discussed above. Recall that the home literacy practices of the families from Roadville and Trackton were different from each other. Moreover, both were different from the home literacy practices of the White middle-class families, which were more closely aligned with the literacy practices of the local schools.

Without taking the time to understand and explore our students' personal and cultural histories as learners, we run the risk of not providing appropriate instruction. What we're teaching, and the manner in which we're teaching, may differ greatly from our students' cultural and linguistic experiences and understandings.

As teachers, we may operate from such different frames of cultural reference that we may not be reaching our students. This can occur when the cultural and linguistic backgrounds of the students and teachers differ vastly and teachers do not realize the importance of understanding these differences rather than viewing them as deficits.

In short, drawing on the work of Vygotsky (1978) and Wertsch (1998), the three teachers in this book hold the following assumptions about learning:

- Student learning is enhanced when teachers strive to understand and base their instruction on the linguistic and cultural backgrounds that children bring to classroom contexts.
- Student learning occurs as a result of effective language-based social interactions in meaningful contexts.
- Student learning is enhanced when teachers (and others, such as peers) provide appropriate scaffolding to support the learning of new concepts and language.

As you enter into the classrooms of Ms. Miller, Mrs. Wood, and Mrs. Weber in Chapters 2–4, you will see how their instructional decisions are based on the three aforementioned assumptions about student learning, as well as their understanding of the importance of acquiring academic English proficiency.

WHAT IS ACADEMIC ENGLISH PROFICIENCY?

In order to progress in school, students need to understand and use academic English. Zwiers (2008) defines academic language as the words and organizational strategies that we use to describe complex ideas and concepts. Teaching academic English supports a student's understanding of the semantic (meaning) and syntactic (rules and patterns) features of language such as vocabulary items, sentence structure, and transition markers. As Scarcella (2003) points out, "Unfortunately, academic English has not been given enough attention in elementary and secondary schools" (p. 16). This lack of attention makes it especially difficult for English learners to comprehend subject-matter content.

To explore what academic English is, we will begin with an example. Please note that the hypothetical situation we describe pertains to teachers in a graduate literacy foundations course. We hope that you, as a teacher, can relate to this example personally because of your own experiences.

At Mountain View University, Drs. Smith and Jones offer separate classes of a foundational graduate course. One of the major tasks in this foundational course is to help graduate students learn to review the professional literature in literacy and write literature reviews. Please read Samples A and B in Figure 1.1 and make notes about the similarities and differences between the two paragraphs.

What did you notice as you read each example? Which of the above samples is an example of the use of academic English in a graduate literacy foundations course, and which is not? Our guess is that you correctly identified Sample B as the example of the use of academic English. Now, what is it about Sample B that makes it an example of academic English? According to Scarcella (2003), there are three dimensions to academic English, a linguistic dimension, a cognitive dimension, and a sociocultural/psychological dimension. We briefly explore each of these dimensions of academic English using the samples in Figure 1.1.

FIGURE 1.1. Samples of the First Paragraph from Two Different Teachers' Papers

Sample A: Teacher 1, Dr. Smith's Class	Sample B: Teacher 2, Dr. Jones's Class
I have been an elementary school teacher for 19 years, and I can sure tell you that the students we teach in our classes have changed a lot over my career. It used to be that all of my children spoke English and came to school with important basic knowledge like the alphabet, beginning reading skills, and so forth. Now, many of my students can barely speak English, and they have trouble with reading and writing in English, too.	Large and growing numbers of children who do not speak English as their first language inhabit U.S. classrooms (Garcia, 2000; Nieto, 2000). For example, Thomas and Collier (2001) estimate that by the year 2040, children who speak a first language other than English will comprise almost 40% of the population of school-aged children in America.

Linguistic Dimension

The linguistic dimension of academic English includes components such as phonology, vocabulary, grammar, and sociolinguistics. English phonology refers to "sounds and the ways these sounds are combined" (Scarcella, 2003, p. 20). Clearly, both Teacher 1 and Teacher 2 in Figure 1.1 understand English phonology. Their spelling indicates that they understand graphemes (symbols) and the ways that graphemes are combined to form correctly spelled words in English.

In order to communicate effectively in English, individuals must know what words mean; that is, they must know English vocabulary. In order "to communicate well in academic settings, it is important to know a large number of academic words" (p. 21). If you look carefully at Samples A and B in Figure 1.1, you undoubtedly will see some differences in vocabulary. For example, Teacher 2 (Sample B) uses words such as *inhabit, estimate,* and *comprise.* Teacher 1 (Sample A) uses different vocabulary—vocabulary that is not consistent with graduate school discourse. For example, she uses "have trouble with" rather than "struggle." The use of academic vocabulary is an indicator of academic English.

Academic English also requires a specialized knowledge of grammar, which is built on a strong understanding of English grammar in more informal contexts. The grammatical component of academic English includes "knowledge of structures—such as passives, parallel clauses, conditionals, and complex clauses" (p. 23).

Finally, the sociolinguistic component of academic English refers to the language user's ability to adjust her writing and/or speaking style "according to the social situation and the topic of discussion" (p. 23). So, for example, Teacher 1 uses the phrase "I can sure tell you" in her writing. This is an example of an inappropriate "style" in formal academic writing. Teacher 2, on the other hand, indicates that there are "large and growing numbers" of English learners in U.S. classrooms, then cites professional references to support this assertion. Next, she provides the reader with a concrete example of what she means by her assertion. This concrete example also is supported with a professional reference. Clearly, Teacher 2 has an understanding of how she should adjust her writing style in a formal academic context.

Cognitive Dimension

The cognitive dimension is the second important dimension of academic English (Scarcella, 2003). This dimension includes components such as background knowledge, the ability to engage in higher-order thinking, and the ability to use strategies to engage with texts. Background knowledge about "ideas, concepts, and definitions" in academic disciplines is a crucial foundation for academic English (Scarcella, 2003, p. 26). Note, for example, that Teacher 2 cites the work of Thomas and Collier (2001) as she provides an example of how the population of English learners is growing in American schools. Academic "insiders" who know about research pertaining to English learners would consider this a powerful citation at this point in the text. Thomas and Collier (2001) conducted an extensive five-year, national, multimillion-dollar, government-funded study to ascertain the situation regarding English learners in the United States. This kind of background knowledge helps Teacher 2 to write a more compelling argument about the value of the work that she is doing.

This reference to Thomas and Collier's work also illustrates the ability of Teacher 2 to engage in higher-order thinking. To craft a persuasive argument for the value/benefit of her review of the literature, Teacher 2 decided to use a highly persuasive piece of evidence (i.e., the Thomas and Collier 2001 study) to provide a rationale for her work.

The third component of the cognitive dimension of academic English is the ability to effectively use strategies such as "underlining, highlighting, paraphrasing in the margins, outlining, . . . identifying key ideas, . . . anticipating and answering questions" (Scarcella, 2003, p. 27). As a concrete example, Teacher 2 knows that sophisticated readers of academic text expect writers to provide concrete examples of the assertions they make in order to craft convincing rationales for their arguments. So, after making the assertion that there are large and growing numbers of English learners in U.S. schools (and citing professional references for this assertion), Teacher 2 drew on the important 2001 research study by Thomas and Collier to provide a specific example of just how many English learners are expected in the United States by the year 2040.

Sociocultural/Psychological Dimension

Scarcella (2003) identifies the sociocultural/psychological dimension as the third and final dimension of academic English. Drawing on the work of Vygotsky (1978) and Gee (1996, 2002), Scarcella (2003) asserts that "academic English arises not just from knowledge of the linguistic code and cognition, but also from social practices in which academic English is used to accomplish communicative goals" (p. 29). These social practices are imbued with norms, values, beliefs, and attitudes. Gee (1996, 1999) refers to these social practices as discourses and makes a distinction between discourse (with a little "d") and Discourse (with a big "D"). For Gee (1999), discourse (with a little "d") refers to language-in-use or the ways that people use oral and written language. Language-in-use involves more than just words. "When 'little d' discourse (language-in-use) is melded integrally with non-language 'stuff' to enact specific identities and activities, then . . . 'big D' Discourses are involved." Discourse (with a capital "D"), then, refers to such things as "one's body, clothes, gestures, actions, interactions, ways of thinking, symbols, tools, technologies . . . , values, attitudes, beliefs, and emotion" (p. 7). Additionally, Gee (1996, 1999) points out that Discourses (with their underlying norms, values, beliefs, and attitudes) are acquired primarily through enculturation or apprenticeship.

Referring to the two teachers in Figure 1.1, a reader rightly might ask, if both teachers were taking the same introductory course in their graduate literacy programs, why is it that Teacher 2 clearly knew more about how to write academic English at the end of her class? A significant part of the answer rests with the different approaches of the professors of the two classes. Dr. Jones (the professor for Teacher 2) designed his course to apprentice his students into the world of the academy. He provided countless models (from his own work as well as the work of his colleagues) of academic writing. He also provided examples of nonacademic writing so that he could teach his students important differences between academic writing and nonacademic writing. He invited former students who had successfully learned to write academic English to talk with his current students and describe their experiences learning academic English. Finally, he provided extensive feedback on his students' evolving papers across the semester as they were learning to write in academic English.

Dr. Smith (the professor for Teacher 1), on the other hand, primarily lectured to his students about writing literature reviews. In the process of his lecturing, he did not provide examples of academic and nonacademic writing. Thus, rather than *apprenticing his students into the process* of understanding about and writing literature reviews, Dr. Smith *lectured his students about* writing literature reviews. Drawing on our earlier comments about learning theory, it is abundantly clear that Dr. Smith did not provide his students with concrete examples of the kinds of writing and thinking he sought to foster in them. Also important, however, Dr. Smith did not scaffold his students' developing understanding of how to actually write appropriate literature reviews.

What do these examples of adult learners have to do with our work in this book focusing on teaching academic English to ELs in elementary school? While the ideas we have presented in these examples are more relevant to adult readers of this book, we wish to emphasize that the process of teaching students to write and speak using academic English is similar for adults and children. Both adults and children benefit from concrete examples of the kinds of writing and speaking the teacher seeks to teach her students. Additionally, both adults and children need meaningful scaffolded instruction that apprentices learners into the process of learning and effectively using academic English.

In the final section of this chapter, we provide additional research-supported examples of how teachers can effectively scaffold the learning of ELs in their classrooms.

RESEARCH-SUPPORTED BEST PRACTICES FOR TEACHING ENGLISH LEARNERS

How do we prepare a literate student population and successfully teach English language skills and academic content to students who come to us from all parts of the world, a variety of socioeconomic strata, and speaking first languages other than English? We address this question by providing a brief review of the research on best practices for effectively teaching ELs in English-speaking classrooms.

The U.S. Department of Education's Institute of Education Sciences considered the challenge of educating ELs to be of the utmost importance and established the National Literacy Panel on Language-Minority Children and Youth (August & Shanahan, 2006). The Panel, consisting of 13 experts from a variety of educational fields (such as second language development and cognitive development), was charged with identifying and synthesizing relevant research literature that focused on the literacy acquisition of English learners in U.S. schools. The major findings from the Panel's work are as follows:

- Instruction that provides substantial coverage of the key components of reading—identified by the National Reading Panel (National Institute of Child Health and Development, 2000) as phonemic awareness, phonics, fluency, vocabulary, and text comprehension—has clear benefits for ELs.
- Instruction toward developing oral proficiency in English, as well as proficiency in the key components of reading, is critical for ELs in order to read and write proficiently in English. Student performance suggests that oral proficiency often is overlooked in instruction.
- Oral proficiency and literacy in the first language can be used to facilitate literacy development in English.
- Individual differences contribute significantly to English literacy development.
- Most assessments do a poor job of gauging individual strengths and weaknesses of ELs.
- There is surprisingly little evidence for the impact of sociocultural variables on literacy achievement or development. However, home language experiences can have a positive impact on literacy achievement (August & Shanahan, 2006, pp. 3–7).

While this Panel's findings support much of the work introduced by the National Reading Panel (National Institute of Child Health and Development, 2000), the main points highlighted by their work, of crucial importance to classroom teachers, and supported by key researchers in the fields of bilingual education and second language acquisition, are the following:

- The need for more oral language experiences in both English and the home language (Cummins, 2000; Krashen, 2004)

- The positive impact of the home language on literacy achievement (Krashen, 2004)
- The importance of texts written in the students' native language (Cummins, 2000)
- The positive impact of culturally relevant text on the learning of English learners (Cummins, 2000)

Drawing on the important research pertaining to ELs just mentioned, as well as the three assumptions about student learning discussed earlier in this chapter, we conclude by sharing three instructional practices that are modeled and discussed throughout Chapters 2–4.

- Best practices for English learners include drawing and building on the linguistic and cultural backgrounds that children bring to classroom contexts.
- Best practices for English learners include providing myriad meaningful opportunities for effective language-based social interactions in the classroom.
- Best practices for English learners include providing effective scaffolding to support their acquiring new language and concepts.

As you read Chapters 2 through 4, please notice that teachers in those chapters draw on the research-supported best practices for ELs that we have presented in this chapter. Additionally, you will see that the instructional practices of each of the three teachers reflect an understanding of the other major conceptual ideas we have presented in this chapter, including learning theory, second language acquisition, academic English, and cross-cultural communication.

CHAPTER 2

Say It Like a Scientist

Designing Science/Literacy Lessons to Support English Learners in First Grade

Maria Grant,
Pamela Cantrell, and Diane Lapp

What makes the sky blue?
Why don't fish sink?
How far is it to the sky?
What do ants eat?
Why don't I have fur like my kitty?
What makes it rain?
What makes leaves crumble when they fall off trees?

QUESTIONS LIKE THESE ARE OFTEN ASKED by young children, who are very interested in the science of themselves and their worlds. This natural curiosity makes science a perfect vehicle through which content information, language, and literacy can be integrated without losing the integrity of any area or the interest of the child.

To see the precision of this integration, we invite you inside Ms. Miller's first-grade classroom, which was introduced in Chapter 1, as she presents a lesson that integrates science, literacy, and academic English. Being well aware of the topical knowledge, language, and literacy differences that exist among her first-grade students, Ms. Miller scaffolds her lessons to accommodate content and literacy growth for each child. Attention to these differences is very important to Ms. Miller because her philosophy of teaching is that in order to grow each child's self-respect as a learner across all of the content areas, her instruction must be engaging and student-centered.

CONCEPTUAL FOUNDATION FOR INSTRUCTION

The instruction that occurs in this classroom involves many collaborative conversations, which Ms. Miller believes is a must if children are going to own the academic language or Discourse of school and the topical language of the various content areas. (See Chapter 1 for a discussion of Discourse; see also Gee, 1996, 1999.) Several of Ms. Miller's students are learning English as an additive language; additionally, they and others are learning academic or school English as a new language register or as a secondary Discourse (Gee, 1996), their first Discourse being their home language or Discourse.

For those who are native English speakers, the ease of learning or adding an academic English register is related to how closely this new school register/Discourse approximates the language/Discourse of their homes. Several children whose home register is Black English need additional support to add the Discourse of school or academic English. As pointed out in Chapter 1, this need is magnified for ELs who are attempting to learn both *conversational language* and *academic language*, or cognitive academic language proficiency, at the same time (Cummins, 1979). To better understand the relationship between these forms of language, let's think about Gee's (1996) description of Discourses.

> Discourses are ways of being in the world, or forms of life which integrate words, acts, values, beliefs, attitudes, and social identities, as well as gestures, glances, body positions, and clothes. A Discourse is a sort of identity kit, which comes complete with the appropriate costume and instructions on how to act, talk, and often write, so as to take on a particular social role that others recognize. (p. 127)

Think about all of your Discourses. The one that is foregrounded at any given time is dependent on the situation and the others with whom you are interacting. As you move from situation to situation, you draw on the Discourse you have for a successful interaction. Have you ever found yourself in a situation, a really important situation, that required a Discourse that you hadn't fully developed? Did you feel anxious and not smart? Many children experience this situation daily in classrooms across the country.

Realizing this, we're sure you can understand why it's so essential that as Ms. Miller designs each lesson, she considers the instructional supports needed by the English speakers whose home and academic Discourses are not too disparate; the children whose home registers, like those of the children whose home Discourses are Black English Vernacular, differ greatly from academic or school English; and finally the children who are learning both conversational and school/academic English as two new Discourses.

Since the focus of this book is the EL, Figure 2.1 has been designed to share an overview of the science, literacy, and academic English concepts that provide the framework for the instruction Ms. Miller presents in the lesson being shared. The instructional supports given to ELs during the lesson also are noted. Now let's learn more about three of these students.

MS. MILLER'S CLASSROOM AND THREE STUDENTS

Ms. Miller teaches in an urban area of San Diego, California. There are 19 children in her first-grade classroom. Ten are ELs, two speak mostly in Black English Vernacular, and seven speak

FIGURE 2.1. Framework for the Integrated Science/Literacy Lesson Addressed in Chapter 2

Category	Conceptual Focus	
Academic language	Negotiating meaning	
Science	Observation and classification Characteristics of living things	
Literacy	Science talk	
	Instructional Approach	*Learning Theory Focus*
English learners	Collaborative conversations	Developing primary and secondary Discourses (Gee, 1996)
	Questioning within the context of scientific investigation	Acquiring vocabulary, connecting background knowledge, and using recently learned content (Zwier, 2008)
	Evidence-based debate and argument	Developing language for the Discourse of scientists
	Scientific inquiry using the 5E Model	Developing scientific reasoning skills (Bybee et al., 2006)

mainstream English—the type of English typically characterized by a particular vocabulary, a narrow range of accents, and specific grammar (Zwiers, 2008). We will focus on three students in Ms. Miller's class.

Susana

Susana is five years old. She emigrated from Mexico when she was just three. At that time, Susana had acquired a significant number of vocabulary words in her native language of Spanish. Susana is close to her grandmother, who has shared the duty of raising her with Susana's mother, with whom she lives. Although she did not attend preschool, Susana was taught by her grandmother to count to 25 and to recite the alphabet in Spanish before she entered kindergarten. Susana attended kindergarten at Ms. Miller's school, but struggled with acquiring both a new oral

language along with the reading and writing skills typically introduced in kindergarten.

Ms. Miller knows that Susana needs opportunities to build both
her everyday ability to communicate with others in her second language of English and her academic language. For this reason, Ms.
Miller intends to provide situations for Susana and her classmates
to generate language through oral conversation as they teach, explain, express, and convince others of the importance of their own
ideas (Zwiers, 2008). This process of conversing with others not
only results in the desired acquisition of language, but also supports students as they gain greater content knowledge.

Asad

Asad, another first-grader in Ms. Miller's class, was born in the
United States. His parents emigrated from Somalia three years before his birth. At home, Asad's family speaks only Somali, but Asad
has learned English simultaneously through his exposure to people
in the community and through his preschool/kindergarten experiences. Ms. Miller occasionally notices that Asad code-switches—that
is, he interjects Somali words into his English-based sentences—
especially when conversing with his friends in casual situations.
When replying to teacher-posed questions in the classroom, Asad
will take time to respond and will select words thoughtfully that he
feels are appropriate. The extensive consideration that Asad feels
he must give to his formal responses often is combined with a sense
of anxiety and apprehension.

Because Asad comes from a home in which a language other
than English is spoken and in which cultural norms differ from
those of mainstream society, he has become acquainted with a Discourse that is different from the Discourse he experiences at school.
Recalling her education classes, Ms. Miller understands that because Asad has been indoctrinated into two somewhat disparate
Discourses, he is using language, symbolic expressions, and "arti-
facts" of thinking, feeling, believing, valuing, and acting that connect him as a member of each of these social groups (Gee, 1996). Ms.
Miller realizes that she can offer Asad support as he accesses the
mainstream Discourse, while still maintaining and respecting the
Discourse that connects him to his family. In fact, Ms. Miller knows
that it is advantageous to develop the ability to fluidly move from
one Discourse to the other in certain situations.

James

James entered Ms. Miller's class one month after the start of the school year. He came to the classroom from a rural community in Georgia and speaks a particular vernacular of Black English. Ms. Miller often notices that James asks his classmates to clarify content information after she initially has explained it. Ms. Miller realizes that she needs to offer James ways to access the language part of literacy, including content vocabulary, grammar, and word pronunciation, along with the sociocultural aspects of mainstream Discourse (Gee, 1996). She knows that literacy is more than simply the acquisition of new words, and that all social groups have culturally based practices that help children in the household develop certain skills. However, only a narrow range of specific skills are valued in schools. Ms. Miller intends to use classroom discussions to help students like James build these skills by allowing them to compare thinking processes and use language in the classroom (Zwiers, 2008). She plans to use questioning to start and maintain discussions and to check for understanding.

THINKING THROUGH THE LESSON DESIGN

As Ms. Miller went through the process of preparing to teach an integrated science/literacy lesson, she drew upon her knowledge of her students, her past graduate and undergraduate coursework, and a variety of other resources, including the Web, to bring together all the elements for a cohesive and effective lesson.

In her literacy studies graduate work, Ms. Miller learned that reading and writing activities are critical to the learning of content—particularly for second language learners (Kamil & Bernhardt, 2004). She reasoned that engaging her students in science learning might be an ideal opportunity to integrate literacy and focus on academic language acquisition as her students learned science content. She was also aware that while the literacy community encourages the use of expository text, the science education community fears that information in science textbooks and trade books will be viewed as science rather than simply *descriptions* of science (Saul, 2004). Therefore, she determined that her students would engage in inquiry science as described in the *National Science Education*

Standards (National Research Council, 1996, 2000) and, at the same time, would "talk and write science in words, and draw, tabulate, graph, geometrize, and algebrize science in all possible combinations" appropriate for their level (Lemke, 2004, p. 41). In her preparation for the lesson, Ms. Miller decided to use the following science concept: *Living things have observable characteristics.* Since it was springtime with new leaves on many trees and plants, and because the class had just completed a science unit on the seasons, she selected leaves as the "living things" the class would investigate as a logical next step in the sequencing of the science content. She knew there would be scientific terms involved in this lesson— *observe, classify, characteristics, same, different, surface, edge, smooth,* and more. In her mind, she sorted through several possible activities and asked herself a number of questions:

1. Is a word search activity that includes science vocabulary really a good way of teaching either science or literacy?
2. Does a trade book with glossy pictures and obscure text written to conform to a specific readability level actually dispel rather than contribute to misconceptions?
3. Does simply reading a trade book that has an animal character (e.g., *The Very Hungry Caterpillar* [Carle, 1987]) actually prompt students to explore their world more carefully and systematically (see Saul, 2004, p. 5)?

She knew that for the integration of science and literacy to be truly powerful, the work undertaken by the students needed to make sense in terms of both disciplines so that neither was subsumed under the other. This would take careful orchestration. She decided that the best approach would be a hands-on activity that would allow students to make observations and then use them as data to classify the leaves. This type of activity would offer solid opportunities for the integration of science and literacy. When students have the opportunity to explore, investigate, and negotiate meaning using firsthand resources such as leaves, talk plays a critical role in making sense of their world. Talk is fundamental to the development of scientific reasoning skills and to the development of theories and explanations. As students talk about the data they have collected and defend their ideas using the data as evidence, they clarify meaning, generate conclusions, and develop new theories (Winokur & Worth, 2006). This process of coming to a mutual understanding through negotiation is a critical element of cultivating academic language acquisition (Zwiers, 2008). Negotiating meaning "means using verbal and nonverbal strategies to interpret, express, expand, and refine many ideas, thoughts, and subtle variations in meaning in a conversation" (Hernandez, 2003, as cited in Zwiers, 2008, p. 43).

As important as talk is to the development of negotiated meaning, talk rarely is taught in school (Calkins, 2000). In thinking about how she would teach appropriate science talk in her classroom to support language development for Susana, Asad, and James, Ms. Miller reviewed some reading material from a content literacy course she had taken during her graduate studies and was reminded that teaching science talk requires specific attention to the

- science content and thinking goals that are the focus of the discussion,
- nature of a classroom culture of science inquiry,
- purpose of the discussion within an inquiry framework,
- stages of a discussion,
- guiding of a discussion, and
- recording of ideas and information (Winokur & Worth, 2006, p. 46)

Ms. Miller also knew that evidence-based debate and argument are important to the scientific reasoning process and are a part of science talk. She recognized that her first-graders would need practice with the appropriate skills, behaviors, and language as they engaged in negotiating meaning. Susana, for instance, could benefit from an offering of sentence starters rooted in the academic language of science. A few appropriate and relevant phrases, provided within the context of a conversation or offered through questioning, could help Susana to move toward scientific inquiry, debate, and summary—all important elements of the scientific reasoning process.

Asad, who is challenged by the fact that he must move between the Discourse of his home and the Discourse of school, would benefit from opportunities to practice having science conversations in partnerships or small groups—arenas that required him to use his new Discourse in a small, safe-feeling situation. Similarly, James, whose Black English Vernacular differs from the mainstream English that is the underpinning of science conversations, is in need of opportunities to first hear and then rehearse using vocabulary and phrasing that are characteristic of science talk. Ms. Miller knows that vocabulary efforts that require James to learn new words, and then use them in various contexts, are critical to the process of fostering a usable acquisition of science language.

To facilitate the kind of learning that Ms. Miller knew was necessary for her students, she would need to explicitly teach the use of specific language for disagreeing respectfully (e.g., "I have a different idea.") and asking for clarification (e.g., "Tell me why you think that."). (See Winokur & Worth, 2006, p. 47.) She decided to incorporate the stages of discussion described in the Talking in Science Framework.

1. Gathering and Taking Stock of Ideas
   a. Setting the stage (What are we wondering about?)
   b. Moving further (What do we think/speculate about this?)
   c. Bringing closure (What are our collective experiences and ideas?)
   d. Encouraging child-to-child discourse—this element is embedded throughout.
2. Planning an Investigation
   a. Setting the stage (What is the question?)
   b. Moving further (How will we find out?)
   c. Bringing closure (What do we predict?)
   d. Encouraging child-to-child discourse—this element is embedded throughout.
3. Developing Conceptual Understanding
   a. Setting the stage (What data do we have?)
   b. Moving further (What do the data say? What claims can we make? What is the evidence to support them?)
   c. Bringing closure (What can we conclude? What new questions do we have?)
   d. Encouraging child-to-child discourse—this element is embedded throughout (Winokur & Worth, 2006, pp. 49–51).

As Ms. Miller thought about the sequence of the lesson, she mentally listed the three skills she hoped to teach during the lesson: observation, classification, and science talk for negotiated meaning. She recognized that a preliminary skill for classification was the ability to distinguish whether leaf characteristics were the same or different when comparing a variety of leaves. She realized that what she hoped to accomplish was a perfect fit with the 5E Instructional Model (Bybee, 2002), widely accepted as an effective model for teaching science in classrooms across the country. The five phases of the 5E Instructional Model include Engage, Explore, Explain, Elaborate, and Evaluate. Teaching the skill of recognizing *same* or *different* characteristics as part of the Engage phase would provide opportunities for students to model and practice science talk and negotiate meaning, thus preparing them to move into the Explore phase and apply these skills in an investigation of their own.

Ms. Miller decided to use trade books as a source of the science content for the Engage phase. Knowing that selecting appropriate books for science sometimes could be tricky, she sought help from the National Science Teachers Association (NSTA) website, which lists outstanding science trade books for K–12 students by year (see http://www.nsta.org/publications/ostb/).

Ms. Miller knew that she wanted books that featured accurate illustrations of plants and animals that could be used for observation and comparison. The text was less important, since her plan was not to use the text except perhaps for identifying the names of organisms if students asked such questions. She found three books on the NSTA website that met her criteria and located them in her school library.

Crocodiles & Alligators (Simon, 2000)
Fabulous Fluttering Tropical Butterflies (Patent, 2003)
National Audubon Society First Field Guide: Trees (Cassie, 1999)

With most of the ideas in mind to prepare her lesson, Ms. Miller gathered a large enough variety of leaves, which were

---

THE INQUIRY QUESTION

Ms. Miller has asked an inquiry question that places the skill of observation using the concepts of same and different into a problem situation. The students must make observations (collect data), analyze the data (decide which characteristics are the same and which are different), and use the results of the analysis to answer the question. Notice how Ms. Miller uses science talk to negotiate meaning and bring closure to the inquiry question.

readily available around the school. She was careful not to permanently damage the plants or trees while collecting. She returned to her classroom with 27 different varieties of leaves, including two types of pine needles and several grasses. At this point, she was ready to make final preparations for the integrated 5E lesson.

SAMPLE INTEGRATED 5E SCIENCE/LITERACY LESSON

Engage

The purpose of the Engage phase is to introduce students to the lesson content using a guided activity. Ms. Miller used the Engage phase to introduce the skills of observation and negotiating meaning through science talk. She was careful not to *tell* the students what the lesson concept was because she wanted them to construct their own understanding as the lesson progressed. Notice as she and the children conversed how she also introduced vocabulary in the context of the lesson rather than teaching the words in isolation. This would aid students in negotiating meaning through science talk.

To start the lesson, Ms. Miller called all the students to sit on the carpet facing her chair. She opened the butterfly book (Patent, 2003) to pages she had preselected, showing several butterflies, and asked students to share what they observed.

- What do you notice?
- How can you describe that characteristic?
- Is there another butterfly on this page with the same characteristic?
- What makes you think that?
- Where did you look to find that out?
- Does anyone have a different idea?
- Which butterfly does not have this characteristic?
- How can you tell?

The conversation continued in this vein until Ms. Miller made sure that all students could identify characteristics that were the same and different and could describe these characteristics accurately.

Ms. Miller showed the cover of the crocodile book (Simon, 2000) and asked the following question: If we were all at the zoo right now and were looking at a pond filled with crocodiles and alligators, how could we tell them apart?

She turned to the preselected pages in the book so the students could make observations, as she asked questions similar to those shown above. When one student observed that some of the animals had teeth showing when the mouth was closed and some did not, she led a discussion about that characteristic.

- Could this be a characteristic that might help us tell an alligator from a crocodile?
- What information (data) do we need to help us answer that question?
- What should we do first to find out?

Susana suggested that they look for more pictures in the book. Because Ms. Miller knew that Susana, in particular, was in need of finding ways to express and convince others of her ideas, she thoughtfully directed related probing questions to the class.

- What information might that add?
- What do you think about that plan?
- What questions do you have for Susana about her plan?

Asad suggested reading the words that described the pictures. Ms. Miller wanted to encourage child-to-child discourse, so she redirected Asad to ask Susana if she would like to add that to her plan, and then prompted Susana to respond respectfully. Both Asad and Susana would benefit from Discourse practice, and Ms. Miller's explicit directives guided them toward this end.

The discussion then continued until Ms. Miller said, "Let's see if we can agree on what our plan will be." The students agreed that it was a good plan to thumb through the book looking for the characteristic of teeth showing or not showing when an animal's mouth is closed and then for Ms. Miller to read aloud the text that talked about the pictures. Once the data gathering was complete, Ms. Miller posed more questions that brought closure to the inquiry question.

- What can we say about the difference between alligators and crocodiles?
- What evidence do we have for that idea?
- What have we learned?

- If we were all back at the zoo looking at the pond filled with alligators and crocodiles, how might we explain the differences between them to someone else?

Before moving on to the next phase of the 5E Instructional Model, Ms. Miller needed to scaffold one more idea so the students would be prepared to complete the leaf classification in the next segment of the lesson as independently as possible. She knew that an important aspect of the classification activity would be student-to-student discourse, so she hoped to introduce explicit respectful language that students would use as they prepared to negotiate meaning. She opened the tree book (Cassie, 1999) and instructed the students that they were going to observe the characteristic of tree shape. She pointed to a tree in the book and asked students to observe carefully and come up with "the best" description of the tree's overall shape. After providing enough time for the students to think, she asked for their responses and received a flood of answers ranging from "a round circle on a stick" to "a tennis racquet," with each student claiming that his or her description was the best.

She then explained to the students that sometimes there is more than one excellent description of something and that when we are working together to decide things, there are respectful ways of talking to each other about ideas. She modeled a conversation with a student, prompting the student to use explicit respectful language. She then asked students to pair and share their ideas using the same respectful language. The first person was to share his or her description of the tree shape, and the second person was directed to say, "Tell me why you think that." The second person then was told to listen carefully while the first person explained. Next the second person would say, "I have an idea that is different from yours." It then was the first person's turn to say, "Tell me why you think that." The pair then had to agree on one of the descriptions or come up with a new description that they could agree on using respectful language. Ms. Miller first modeled this procedure, then gave the pairs time to practice. After reporting on their experiences, Ms. Miller asked students to trade partners and repeat the activity with a new tree shape until she was sure all students were confident with the student-to-student discourse. For Susana, Asad, and James, this was an opportunity to practice both the target Discourse and the skill of scientific reasoning using prompts that scaffolded the language of their conversations.

Explore

The purpose of the Explore phase is to allow students to test their ideas as independently as possible through their own experiences. The role of the teacher in this phase is to support instead of direct student learning, once the inquiry question has been posed.

To begin the Explore phase, Ms. Miller directed the children to return to their tables and listen for the next set of instructions. She explained that since the students had learned how to observe and identify characteristics of living things pictured in nature books, they were now going to collect some living things—leaves—from the schoolyard and bring them back to their classroom for more investigation. Each table of four students was to work together as a group during the collection process. Each member was to collect five leaves from different plants so that when they returned to the classroom, each group would have 20 different leaves. In order to teach the children to be respectful of nature by not damaging the shrubs, Ms. Miller modeled how to carefully pinch off one leaf at a time at the point where the leaf was attached to the branch. She watched the children carefully as they proceeded and prompted them as necessary.

Once the students returned to the classroom, they spread the leaves out on their tables, and Ms. Miller handed each group three

---

INQUIRY LESSONS

Remember that the inquiry question places the science content—this time, characteristics of living things—into a problem situation. Inquiry lessons are organized around inquiry questions and range from guided inquiry—when the teacher defines the inquiry questions and guides the process—to full inquiry, when the students have a more prominent role in making decisions about the process. *Inquiry and the National Science Education Standards* (National Research Council, 2000) presents an inquiry continuum that describes the essential features of classroom inquiry and their variations.

string loops. She instructed the students to shape one loop into a circle on their tables and then place all their leaves inside it. She then had the students make two more circles using the string loops and place them side-by-side below the first circle. She then posed the inquiry question: What leaf characteristic can you use to classify your leaves into two groups?

After stating the inquiry question, Ms. Miller made sure students understood that all the leaves in their collections that had the selected characteristic (same) would be moved to one of the empty circles, and all those without the characteristic (different) would be moved to the second empty circle. Ms. Miller knew that Asad would benefit from learning about the process of classification through the use of the circles. Additionally, she planned for a situation in which he would participate in a conversation with four other people in a way that would allow him the extra time he needed to process the language and would provide the opportunity to hear other students present examples using the target Discourse.

Before starting, Ms. Miller called on students to share their ideas of what should be done first (make observations), and what came next (agree on a characteristic), and what came after that (classify leaves into two groups—one with and one without the characteristic), and to use respectful language as they made decisions together.

Ms. Miller circulated the room noting that groups were using broad characteristics such as size, color, and shape. One group identified their characteristic as "like a hand." When she asked them to tell her more detail, they explained that some of the leaves had "shapes kind of like fingers going out from the main part" (lobes), while others did not. She continued around the room asking groups to explain their observations and evidence for classifying the leaves the way they did, and prompting students to use explicit language as they negotiated meaning. She assisted one group with their characteristic of "big" by helping them understand that they needed to express a qualifier such as "bigger than _____." When Ms. Miller visited Susana's group, she noticed that Susana was struggling to express and defend her ideas—an area in which Susana commonly needed guidance and practice. In response to her observation, Ms. Miller prompted Susana to articulate her reasoning when moving a leaf into an empty circle: "Why did you decide to move that leaf into that circle?" In response, Susana explained, "The outside part of the leaf is like the outside of the others in that circle." Susana ran her finger along the border of the leaf as she described it and pointed to similar leaves to justify her decision. When all groups had completed the task, the class was ready to move to the next phase of the lesson.

Explain

The purpose of the Explain phase is for students to make conceptual sense of the science content explored in the previous activity. Ms. Miller began this phase by asking the groups to share their classifications. By doing so, she could note any misconceptions that may have arisen and formalize science vocabulary and literacy skills. Science talk is also important here, so many of the questions used previously are incorporated into this phase as well.

As the class gathered around the first table, Ms. Miller asked groups to share their classifications.

- What do you observe about this group's classification?
- What evidence do you have about that idea?
- Where did you look to find that evidence?
- Does anyone have a different idea?
- What would you like to ask or say to the group about their characteristic?
- What would you like to ask or say to the group about their classification?

Ms. Miller encouraged students to make statements or pose questions such as, "If this leaf has the characteristic, why doesn't that one?" This type of question calls on the group members to defend their stance using evidence. When it came time for James to ask questions and comment on the work of a presenting group, Ms. Miller noticed that he hesitated when trying to formulate a thought. She prompted him by asking him to compare his own group's classification with that of the presenting group—"How are they different? How are they the same?" James, now given a jump-start, proceeded to discuss how his group chose color as a way to decide which circle to place a leaf in, and the presenting group used size. "This is how our groups are different," he noted. Ms. Miller's prompt was intended to both scaffold his use of the language and build his confidence when participating in science talk within the classroom.

FIGURE 2.2. Initial Version of Asad's Group's Chart

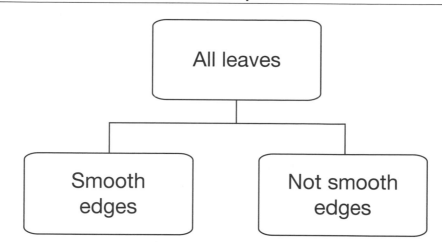

As the groups continued to share their work, Ms. Miller started a chart for each one that modeled their classification system. She wrote the characteristics displayed by the group's classification at the top of each chart: smooth edges, long and pointed, shiny on top, hand-shaped, and bigger than my hand. Asad's group's chart is shown in Figure 2.2.

Once each group had shared and discussed its classification, Ms. Miller closed this phase of the lesson by checking for conceptual understanding:

THE IMPORTANCE OF VISUALS

Ms. Miller is building a visual representation of each group's data using a binary (yes/no) classification system. Scientists use binary systems, or dichotomous keys, to identify organisms. When using a dichotomous key, a scientist compares one characteristic, such as leaf edges, with a visual and written description in the key. If the scientist answers "yes," meaning the leaf edge is as described in the key, she is directed to a different characteristic. If she answers "no," she is directed to a visual and written description of a different leaf edge, and the process starts over again. So this activity exposes these first-grade students to an important scientific process that uses visual information to make decisions.

- What have we learned about the characteristics of living things so far?
- How does careful observation help us identify the characteristics of living things?
- What were some of the characteristics we used to classify the leaves into two groups?

Elaborate

The purpose of the Elaborate phase is to provide students with a new activity that allows them to apply the lesson concept in a slightly different context that will expand their conceptual understanding. Ms. Miller began this phase by explaining to the students that sometimes scientists use tools to help them observe. After asking students to name any such tools they could think of, she distributed a hand lens to each student and provided each group with two additional string loops. She instructed the students to practice with the lenses using leaves from the circle that did *not* have their selected characteristic. The leaves that showed their previously selected characteristic were to remain in place inside the string circle.

Ms. Miller allowed students to experiment with the new tool for about five minutes, then posed a series of questions.

- How might this tool help us in finding new characteristics?
- What characteristics could you see through the lens that you could not see very well with just your eyes?

EXTENDING CONCEPTUAL UNDERSTANDING

Each group's binary classification chart is now a multilevel chart, thus extending the conceptual understanding that living organisms can be classified using more than one characteristic. It will be important for Ms. Miller to ask appropriate questions of the students that guide their thinking toward the extended concept and allow them to verbalize the concept and connect it with the evidence from their charts. Ms. Miller also could differentiate this activity by inviting those students who would like an additional challenge to complete the two empty boxes on row 3.

Students named several new characteristics: hairy back, edges that look like sharp teeth, blood veins, skin like an orange, and tiny straight lines (parallel veins as in grasses). She accepted all answers at face value and did not comment on the fact that while leaves do have veins, they are not filled with blood. She would address that at a later time.

Ms. Miller then posed the inquiry question: What new characteristic can you use to classify the leaves from your old characteristic into two new groups? Ms. Miller instructed the students to place the two new string loops as side-by-side circles below the circle showing their old characteristic. As before, Ms. Miller circulated the room and checked in with the students. She asked clarifying questions about their selected characteristic and prompted them to use respectful language. When Ms. Miller got to James's group, she found James leading his classmates as they divided the leaves by vein structure. As hoped, the previously offered guided prompts and encouraged practice bolstered James's confidence in a way that fostered his ability to take the lead in this later stage of the 5E process.

When the groups completed the task, Ms. Miller followed the same format as before. The students shared their results, asking questions of one another. Ms. Miller made sure that students defended their classification system with evidence they could verbalize. She added a new level to each group's chart. The addition to Asad's group's chart is shown in Figure 2.3.

FIGURE 2.3. Final Version of Asad's Group's Chart

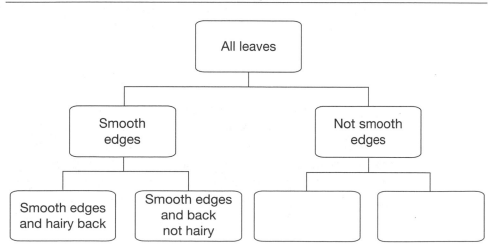

To complete the lesson, Ms. Miller asked the students from each group to select one leaf as an example of the characteristic in each box in rows 2 and 3 of their charts and to tape it in the appropriate box. She then checked for conceptual understanding.

- What have we learned about the characteristics of living things today?
- How did using the hand lenses help us identify additional characteristics of living things?
- What were some of the new characteristics we used to classify the leaves into two groups using the hand lenses?
- How many different characteristics did different groups use to classify the leaves?
- Why might it be a good thing to use more than one characteristic to classify a living thing?

Evaluate

Ms. Miller assessed student performance during every phase of the lesson. Prior to starting the lesson, she prepared a checklist of her students' names listed in the rows and observable behaviors associated with the skills and concepts presented in the lesson in the columns of a grid. She carried the checklist with her throughout the lesson and checked appropriate boxes for students as she observed the targeted behaviors. She also noted the degree of correctness of group choices of leaves that were taped on the charts.

The Evaluate phase of the lesson can serve as a summative assessment of what students know and can do at this point. Evaluation also can be embedded throughout all of the other phases, as Ms. Miller did in this lesson.

FINAL THOUGHTS

This sample lesson demonstrates how the following learning objectives can be targeted alongside the instruction of new science content: vocabulary acquisition, language development for the purpose of scientific Discourse, and the augmentation of scientific reasoning skills. Ms. Miller clearly understood the particular needs of the students in her class, including those designated as ELs. The lesson allowed her students to concentrate on the tenets of scientific inquiry and oral language while simultaneously focusing on the concepts of classification and organization.

When Ms. Miller noticed that Susana was struggling with expressing and defending her opinions, she prodded Susana with questions that would frame the language and would direct her thoughts. Asad, whose challenge is moving from a familial Discourse to classroom science talk, was provided with small-group opportunities to engage in conversations that offered peer modeling and time for gathering thoughts before articulation—both critical pieces in Asad's growing ability to participate in a new Discourse. For James, learning new science words through context and oral language offered a depth of understanding that far exceeds what typically is acquired when students merely look up and record dictionary definitions for new terms.

Ms. Miller incorporated the 5E Instructional Model (Bybee, 2002) as a foundation for modeling scientific inquiry. She thoughtfully integrated oral language instruction into the phases of the 5E model: Engage, Explore, Explain, Elaborate, and Evaluate.

For the Engage phase of the lesson, students were presented with trade book visuals and were asked to make observations. Vocabulary was accessed within the context of the illustrations to provide greater meaning and relevance. To allow students to Explore, the second phase of the 5E model, students, working in teams of four, classified leaves. To successfully complete this task, they had to negotiate language that was inquiry-based and descriptive. Students had to describe characteristics of leaves and determine categories for *same* and *different* classifications. To proceed to the Explain phase, Ms. Miller asked her students to present their ideas for leaf classification. She also required students to comment and question peers in a process of clarification. Again the tenets of scientific talk were employed as students asked for justifications and scientific reasoning from their classmates. As a part of the Elaborate phase, students extended their understanding of science by incorporating a tool, a hand lens, which allowed them to further explore classification. Once again, negotiation using the Discourse of science was a requirement. Finally, to Evaluate, Ms. Miller utilized a checklist throughout the lesson. This method of assessment allowed her to pinpoint areas of specific need for individual students. She then could know where and when to reteach certain topics or skills and was provided with a way to assess the effectiveness of her own instruction.

Throughout the lesson, Ms. Miller noted the behaviors and needs of her ELs. Her specific actions were used intentionally to scaffold language and provide opportunities for students like Susana, Asad, and James to grow in both their knowledge of science content and their use of science language. Language development within the context of a challenging and word-heavy content area, like science, is difficult for any learner. For ELs, those simultaneously taking on the acquisition of a second language, it's a challenge that requires the concerted effort and support of a skilled and thoughtful educator.

CHAPTER 3

Figure It Like a Mathematician

Integrating Mathematics and Literacy to Support English Learners in Third Grade

CYNTHIA BROCK,
LYNDA WIEST,
RACHEL SALAS, AND
DIANNA TOWNSEND

D O YOU FIND THAT JUST AS your English learners are feeling success because they are able to compute addition and subtraction problems, their self-esteem is quickly diminished when you ask them to read and complete a word problem that calls for the same calculations but includes words that are unfamiliar to them? This is an example of the situation addressed by Mrs. Wood as she and her students engaged in a problem-solving lesson pertaining to the topic of exponential growth.

In this chapter, we invite you inside Mrs. Wood's third-grade classroom, which was introduced in Chapter 1, as she presents a lesson to her students that is designed to support integrated mathematics, literacy, and academic language learning for all students, especially ELs. The mathematics, literacy, and academic English concepts to be addressed in this chapter are identified in Figure 3.1. Also illustrated are the instructional supports, with their theoretical foundations, that Mrs. Wood provides to the ELs during the lesson. Although we discuss each of the categories shown in Figure 3.1 within the context of the sample lesson, we highlight learning academic English. As we explained in Chapter 1, academic English refers to the words and organizational strategies that are used to describe complex ideas and concepts in school subjects (Zwiers, 2008) and is often a stumbling block for English learners. Now let's find out more about the three focus ELs in Mrs. Wood's classroom.

Figure 3.1. Framework for Third-Grade Integrated Mathematics/Literacy Lesson

Category	Conceptual Focus	
Academic language	Supporting points with evidence Concept of doubling	
Mathematics	Problem solving Exponential growth	
Literacy	Narrative story structure	
	Instructional Approach	*Learning Theory Focus*
	Language objectives and language support (in Spanish and English)	Effective social interactions
English learners	Building background knowledge	Scaffolding
	Use of visuals and hands-on materials	Scaffolding
	Engaging in collaborative discussion (with peers and teacher)	Scaffolding and effective social interactions

MRS. WOOD'S CLASSROOM
AND THE THREE FOCUS ENGLISH LEARNERS

You may recall that Mrs. Wood—a teacher for eight years—is a third-grade European American teacher in a small community near Portland, Oregon. She teaches in a school with an ESL teacher, but her school district does not have a bilingual education program. Mrs. Wood has 26 students in her class. Two-thirds of these students are monolingual English-speaking European American children. The remaining one-third are Latino and speak Spanish as their first language.

In this chapter we highlight three ELs in Mrs. Wood's classroom. Their backgrounds are described below, as well as Mrs. Wood's thinking about how to plan lessons to accommodate each of these children's learning needs.

Homero

Because Spanish is Homero's first language, Mrs. Wood assumes that he is fluent in oral Spanish for his age level. However, because Mrs. Wood's school district does not have a bilingual education program, Homero never received formal instruction or assessment in Spanish. Homero reads at the fifth-grade level in English, and he speaks and writes fluently in English. Mrs. Wood's ongoing concern—especially when planning whole-class lessons—is whether the work is challenging enough for Homero, who is her top academic student in all areas.

Homero, the oldest of four children, was born in Oregon and has always attended schools there. He travels back and forth to Mexico several times each year with his family to visit extended family. Mrs. Wood has noticed that Homero often assumes a leadership role in the classroom and on the playground.

Adriana

Adriana attended school in Mexico during first, second, and part of third grade (the family just recently moved to Oregon). Adriana is one of six children. She and her family live with Homero, who is her first cousin. Her immediate family and extended family speak Spanish at home. A conversation with Adriana's family revealed that she was a successful student in Mexico. This is great news to Mrs. Wood. This means that Adriana learned important literacy and academic skills in Spanish that Mrs. Wood can build upon and help her transfer to English. Mrs. Wood knows that it is much easier for ELs to learn literacy and academic skills in English when they have learned these skills in another language (Thomas & Collier, 2001). She also knows, however, that it can take a minimum of five to seven years, or more, to become proficient in a new language (Thomas & Collier, 2001; see also August & Shanahan, 2006). Mrs. Wood will have to provide extensive and ongoing support in her lessons and classroom structure for Adriana because she is beginning the English acquisition process and at the beginning level in learning to read, write, and speak in English.

Gabriela

Gabriela, the middle child in a family of three children, was in first grade and just starting to learn to read and write in Spanish when her family moved to the United States from Guatemala. Thus, Gabriela did not develop many literacy skills in her native Spanish that could transfer to her English literacy learning. Mrs. Wood realizes that Gabriela needs much scaffolding and careful instruction because she is trying to learn English literacy and academic skills while she is trying to learn to speak English. Gabriela is about a year and a half into the long and arduous process of becoming proficient in English. Gabriela is reading near the end of the first-grade level in English. While it may seem that Gabriela is ahead of Adriana in the development of her English skills, Adriana had a solid foundation of Spanish reading and writing to build upon and transfer to English, so it is likely that Adriana's English reading, writing, and speaking skills may surpass Gabriela's during the year (Thomas & Collier, 2001).

PREPARATION FOR AN INTEGRATED LESSON

Over the past few years, Mrs. Wood has begun to develop more and more integrated lessons because she believes from her observations, her reflections about her instruction, and her graduate studies that students' learning is deepened and enhanced if academic concepts are addressed in meaningful, integrated ways (Bruner, 1996). As a consequence she also has found that meaningful integration of school subjects is time-efficient (Gavelek, Raphael, Biondo, & Wang, 2000). This latter practical reason for integrating subjects was especially compelling to Mrs. Wood given increased curricular demands in already-packed school days. Mrs. Wood was aware, however, of potential problems with integrating academic subjects. For example, if integrated lessons are not carefully designed, teachers may address important academic concepts superficially in the subjects they seek to integrate (Gavelek et al., 2000). Mrs. Wood kept all of these factors in mind as she planned the integrated mathematics/literacy lesson we share with you in this chapter.

This lesson focuses on the children's book *One Grain of Rice: A Mathematical Folktale* (Demi, 1997). A central goal of the lesson was to build academic language skills that would help the children understand the vocabulary, as well as the mathematics and literacy concepts, that would be addressed relative to the story. Because Mrs. Wood was particularly concerned with ensuring that her English learners understood as much of the lesson as possible, she planned preliminary activities for them and structured her whole-class lesson to have Prereading, During-Reading, and Postreading components that included math and literacy skills and strategies as well as academic English skills (Fitzgerald & Graves, 2004; Zwiers, 2008). Recognizing the contribution partner work can make to student learning, especially for ELs, Mrs. Wood flexibly groups her children in dyads. These dyads change across time as children's needs, and the projects on which they are working, change. Mrs. Wood posts dyad lists on the classroom wall so her children always know their current partners and can pair quickly with study buddies when asked.

Building Background Knowledge

Before starting the whole-group lesson, Mrs. Wood built her ELs' knowledge and language bases by asking the bilingual classroom assistant, Mrs. Ruiz, to do some small-group "Before-Story" work with Adriana, Gabriela, and several other English learners. Mrs. Wood is fortunate to have Mrs. Ruiz come to her class three times a week for several hours.

As previously outlined in Figure 3.1, two important concepts that Mrs. Wood and Mrs. Ruiz planned to develop were exponential growth (mathematics) and narrative story structure (literacy). In

---

TEACHING EXPONENTIAL GROWTH

Mrs. Wood made an appropriate decision to focus on exponential growth in this lesson. Third grade is the level at which students start to show intuitive knowledge of the difference between linear growth and exponential (or non-linear) growth (Ebersbach & Wilkening, 2007). Therefore, it is developmentally appropriate to address this concept formally in third grade. In fact, it is important for teachers to provide such instruction to make children's developing intuitive knowledge (of topics such as exponential growth) more explicit. Further, even though algebraic concepts—such as exponential growth—are part of the national mathematics standards for Grades K–12, they typically are underaddressed at the elementary level.

---

order to understand the notion of exponential growth, the students would need to understand the word *doubling* and the mathematics concept that doubling represents. So, prior to reading the story, Mrs. Ruiz taught the concept of doubling in Spanish and English as it related to the story. Additionally, Mrs. Ruiz had the children use manipulatives across the span of four to five days to illustrate how doubling works.

Because the class had studied narrative story structure in the past, Mrs. Ruiz referred the ELs to two wall charts outlining narrative story structure. (One chart was in Spanish, and one was in English.) As the children reflected on the charts, Mrs. Ruiz discussed a story the children had read recently and reminded them about the setting and characters, the rising action in the story, the turning point, the falling action, and the resolution. She then invited them to think about the structure of the story that she was about to read.

Introducing the Story in Spanish

Mrs. Wood was able to get a Spanish translation of *One Grain of Rice* (Demi, 1997). Whenever possible, Mrs. Wood acquires both Spanish and English versions of the books she uses in class. Because Mrs. Ruiz had worked with many translated stories, she was aware that translations are not always accurate. Consequently, when she used Spanish translations of English texts, she always checked them ahead of time for accuracy. After doing this preparation, Mrs. Ruiz read the Spanish translation of the story aloud to the ELs and discussed the story with them. Mrs. Ruiz also helped the children write key vocabulary words from the story (e.g., *raja*) in their journals in both Spanish and English. The children then wrote "kid-friendly" definitions (Beck, McKeown, & Kucan, 2002) in both languages. By doing all of this preliminary work in Spanish with Mrs. Ruiz, the children gained important background knowledge of the story, as well as important conceptual and language knowledge, that they would need to draw upon when Mrs. Wood read the book in English. Now let us share with you Mrs. Wood's integrated lesson.

SAMPLE INTEGRATED MATHEMATICS/LITERACY LESSON

Prereading Activities

Mrs. Wood started the first whole-class part of the lesson by asking her students to imagine that they had won a contest where they could choose one of two prizes: (1) a quarter, or (2) one penny on the first day of the week, two pennies on the second day, four on the third, and so on, for a five-day period. Mrs. Wood made sure that the children knew what she meant by "penny" and "quarter" before she posed the problem. She told the students that a penny was one cent and that a quarter was the equivalent of 25 cents. She showed the children actual coins to make sure that they know what the labels "penny" and "quarter" stood for.

Mrs. Wood then asked the children to pair with their study buddies and discuss which prize they would prefer and why. After giving the children several minutes to talk, Mrs. Wood asked for

---

Problem Solving

Mrs. Wood was wise to focus on problem solving in this target lesson. First, problem solving tends to be difficult for children, so it is important for them to have plenty of practice with it (National Council of Teachers of Mathematics, 2000). Second, problem solving is an important mathematics standard that should be stressed at all school levels, including with younger students like third-graders (National Council of Teachers of Mathematics, 2000).

volunteers to share their choices and explain their reasoning. She next asked them to write their predictions in their journals with their reason(s) for their decision. Mrs. Wood informed the children that a character in the story that they would be reading (a king in India—called a *raja*) would face a similar situation. Mrs. Wood said, "As you listen to the story, listen for the similar situation and see if you can identify it."

Mrs. Wood told the students that they were going to talk about the story for a few minutes before she started reading it to them. She invited them to come to the story carpet quietly and sit next to their study buddies. (The story carpet in Mrs. Wood's classroom is a large area rug near the front of her classroom with a rocking chair.) Once the children were seated on the story carpet, Mrs. Wood shared the title of the book (i.e., *One Grain of Rice: A Mathematical Folktale*) aloud and said the story was a folktale from India. She reminded the children about several folktales they had already read together and asked them to discuss folktale characteristics with their study buddies. Once the class debriefed about the major characteristics—

THE IMPORTANCE OF STRONG FEMALE CHARACTERS

It is significant that the main character of *One Grain of Rice* is an intelligent female. With respect to gender stereotyping in children's books, Sadker and Sadker (1995) emphasize that things have improved, but that "representation is far from equal, and starkly drawn stereotypes remain: competitive, creative, and active boys; dependent, submissive, and passive girls" (p. 260). Giorgis and colleagues (2000) describe the need for strong female characters in children's books this way: "It is important that all readers find themselves in the books that they read. It is equally important that readers discover characters that break stereotypes and serve as role models. Strong female characters can be those from the past or the present. What makes them admirable is their ability to solve problems, overcome adversity, and persevere when circumstances within society present overwhelming obstacles" (p. 521). Educators are in positions of great influence with regard to reading material available to and chosen by young people. Both girls and boys need to see females portrayed in a variety of roles, especially ones showing girls as strong, active problem solvers. This is particularly important with the current emphasis on teaching other content areas, such as mathematics, through the use of children's literature.

which included that they are stories that have been told for a long time about the lives of "folk"—Mrs. Wood told them that they were going to be reading a folktale that was set in India. As she spoke she wrote on the whiteboard: "Setting = India many years ago." She asked for a volunteer to show where India was located on the large world map posted on the classroom wall. She also asked another volunteer to find Portland, Oregon, and show how far they were from India, where the story took place. Each volunteer placed a "sticky flag" on the location she found. Then Mrs. Wood used a string to connect the two locations. This way, the children had a visual that they could refer to during and after the story. Mrs. Wood then said and wrote the following on the whiteboard: "Characters = Rani (a wise girl who taught an important lesson to her leader) and *raja* (a leader, like a king, in India, the country where Rani lived)."

Next Mrs. Wood reminded the children that narratives follow a typical format or structure. She used the overhead projector to share the structure and asked the class to think about their favorite stories and help her fill in the main parts of a "typical" narrative story structure (see Figure 3.2). After they had reviewed the structure, they filled in the setting (India) and characters' names for the focus story. Next Mrs. Wood shared the cover of the book with the children and shared several key pictures throughout the story to give the children a visual sense of the storyline of the book (Díaz-Rico & Weed, 2002). She then asked the children to think about the setting, characters, and pictures, and to turn to their study buddies and make a prediction about the plot of the story. She told the children that they would be completing the story structure chart once they finished and discussed the story.

FIGURE 3.2. Narrative Story Structure

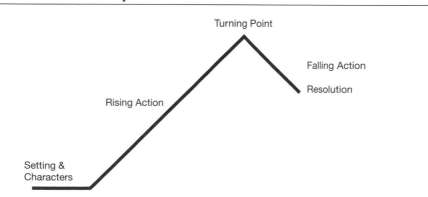

Turning Point

Falling Action

Resolution

Rising Action

Setting &
Characters

During-Reading Activities

Mrs. Wood read the story aloud to the children. In case you haven't read *One Grain of Rice,* it's about a prosperous region in India long ago. The *raja* of the region collected taxes (in the form of rice) from his subjects during each harvest. Over the years he gathered a great surplus of stored rice. Then the weather conditions changed, and the rice harvests were no longer abundant. Many people in the region were starving, but the *raja* had plenty of rice in his vast storehouses. One day as rice was being transported from the storehouses to the *raja's* castle, some rice was lost beside the road due to a tear in one of the bags. A young girl named Rani

---

USING STORIES TO TEACH MATHEMATICS

Mrs. Wood asked her children to begin the problem-solving process in the context of reading and discussing a compelling children's book, *One Grain of Rice* (Demi, 1997). A story is "compelling" if it is sufficiently rich and engaging; sometimes books written solely to "teach" mathematics concepts are not (Harniss, Carnine, Silbert, & Dixon, 2002). Scholars have emphasized the benefits of using quality children's literature to foster children's mathematical growth when the mathematics problems are couched in exciting and/or engaging story contexts (Moschkovich, 2007). Notice how Demi embeds mathematics in a real-world scenario that is reasonably authentic, and that the story was set in a cultural context other than the United States.

During the shared reading, Mrs. Wood made sure that the class interactively but briefly discussed the rising action, turning point, falling action, and resolution to the story. However, Mrs. Wood believes firmly that too much instruction and stopping during a read-aloud can detract from children's interest in and enjoyment of a story, so she took care to minimize interruptions to the flow of the story as she read it aloud. Through the brief discussions, the children determined that the *rising action* was the part of the story leading up to the *raja's* gift to Rani. The *turning point* included Rani's request for the rice and the *raja's* decision to give Rani the gift she requested. The *falling action* occurred as the *raja* and his servants realized that Rani's request would deplete the *raja's* storehouses of rice. The *resolution* involved Rani giving the rice to her starving fellow countrymen and the *raja's* realization that he had been stingy and selfish and needed to become more giving, like Rani.

NARRATIVE STORY STRUCTURE

The most important literacy concept that Mrs. Wood addressed in her lessons was narrative story structure. Our lives are infused with narratives—both the stories we live and the stories we tell and write (Bruner, 1986). In Western culture, narratives assume a typical structure—rising action, turning point, falling action, and resolution (Labov & Waletzky, 1967). While exposure to hundreds of stories during childhood, including the years before entering school, can help children to intuitively internalize this typical story structure, making this "invisible" structure explicit for children can foster children's literacy learning in important ways (Cunningham, 2000; Heath, 1991). For example, not all children hear hundreds of stories prior to coming to school; consequently, these children will not have had a chance to internalize the typical narrative story structure. Making this typical narrative story structure explicit is important because an understanding of story structure helps children to comprehend stories (Kamil, Mosenthal, Pearson, & Barr, 2000). That is, by understanding story structure, children know what to expect when they are hearing, reading, and writing stories. They come to expect stories to "behave" in particular ways.

began collecting the fallen rice. When the *raja's* servants saw Rani collect the rice, they took her before the *raja* and told him that she was stealing his rice. Rani told the *raja* that she was not stealing his rice; rather, she was collecting it from the road to return to him. The *raja* told her that he appreciated her honesty and loyalty. He said that he would reward her with any gift she requested. Her request was the following: "I would like one grain of rice the first day, and then double that amount each day thereafter for 30 days." (Because Rani's request was the exponential problem the children needed to understand, Mrs. Wood had written it out on a sentence strip and posted it on the whiteboard so that the class could refer to the central problem later when they discussed the story.) The *raja* pondered Rani's request and then agreed to it, saying that it did not seem like a very substantial gift. However, as the *raja's* servants gave Rani the requested rice each day, they learned that toward the end of the 30 days, the *raja's* storehouses of rice were almost depleted. Rani shared the rice with her poor and starving countrymen. When the *raja* learned that Rani's request had almost completely depleted his storehouses of rice, but that Rani gave the rice to her starving fellow countrymen, he was impressed with her good deed. He told Rani that she served as a good role model of kindness and generosity to the *raja* as well as to all the people of the land. The *raja* vowed to change his ways and become more benevolent.

Postreading Activities

After reading the story, Mrs. Wood asked the children to return to their desks. She led the class in completing the story structure chart using the document camera. Students listed the story events that represented each phase of the story structure chart. Mrs. Wood was careful to model to her students how to use events from the story itself to construct a rationale for why they believed that the story was structured as they proposed.

Mrs. Wood next asked the children to take out their journals and write answers to the following questions using evidence from the story:

1. Do you think Rani made a good decision in her request to the *raja*? Why or why not?
2. [if not addressed with previous question] If you were Rani, what choice would you make and why?
3. Why do you think the amount of rice Rani received grew so fast in 30 days?

Mrs. Wood discussed the questions orally with the class to make sure everyone understood the questions they were to address in their journals. She also modeled how they might answer the first question by drawing on evidence from the story. She gave the children 10 to 12 minutes to write their answers to the remaining questions, reminding the children to draw on evidence from the story to support their interpretations.

With the exception of Adriana, most of Mrs. Wood's English learners understood both Spanish and English (although they were at different levels of proficiency in both languages). However, because Mrs. Wood had the questions written only in English, and Adriana spoke solely Spanish, Mrs. Wood asked Homero to translate the questions into Spanish orally for Adriana as she worked through answering the three questions. Adriana and Homero knew that Adriana could ask multiple times for translations as she needed them, because hearing translations just once

> ### DRAWING ON EVIDENCE
>
> As explained in Chapter 1, academic language can be defined as the words and organizational strategies that we use to describe complex ideas and concepts (Zwiers, 2008). Supporting points with evidence is an important feature of academic language that Mrs. Wood focused on in her lesson. One way Mrs. Wood focused on this academic language feature was by requiring her children to support their story interpretations with evidence. For example, when children offered interpretations of the story during group discussion time, Mrs. Wood asked them to explain what evidence they drew upon from the text for their interpretations. Also, when she assigned journal-writing tasks, she explicitly asked the children to provide evidence from the text, in writing, for their interpretations. Thus, in Mrs. Wood's class it isn't sufficient to just say or write, "This is my interpretation." Rather, children must say or write, "This is my interpretation because . . . and the evidence from the story that I base my interpretation on is . . ."

might not be sufficient to fully understand the questions. Adriana wrote her answers in Spanish.

After the children had written in their journals, Mrs. Wood asked them to join their study buddies. She paired two groups of study buddies together to form groups of four. The children shared their thoughts from their journals with one another. Mrs. Wood made sure that English learners (like Adriana) were paired with bilingual children, so each group of four had translators. She stated explicitly that children were invited to speak in Spanish or English during the small-group discussions. She asked children who were bilingual in each group to translate, if necessary, for monolingual children in the group. After giving the children several minutes to discuss their answers to the three questions, Mrs. Wood asked each group to find a fair way to choose a spokesperson to report some of the group's key ideas. As Mrs. Wood read each question in turn, group spokespersons shared their ideas for others to respond to, if interested. The children who were bilingual translated from Spanish to English and English to Spanish as needed during the discussion.

After the class discussion, Mrs. Wood asked the children to return to their dyads to complete a mathematics activity pertaining to the story. She reminded the children of the question that she had posed to them before the story. (As a reminder, the question was as follows: Imagine that you won a contest where you could choose one of two prizes: (1) a quarter, or (2) one penny on the first day of the week, two pennies on the second day, four on the third, and so on, for a five-day period.) She asked the children to think back to the prize that they initially had chosen and why. She handed each dyad a chart with blank areas for each day of the week as well as plastic coins. She asked the children in each dyad to work together to determine whether they would want Prize 1 or Prize 2.

As the children finalized their work, Mrs. Wood mentioned that she would be asking at least one study buddy dyad to share its work and thinking with the rest of the class. Homero and Adriana were paired as study buddies. Mrs. Wood paired these two children because she knew that Homero could help his cousin, Adriana, with translation between English and Spanish and conceptual ideas the class covered in all subject areas. As Mrs. Wood taught various subjects and concepts to her class, however, she often checked Homero's understanding of academic concepts because she wanted to make sure that he understood the class content before translating for Adriana. Mrs. Wood was also aware that Homero was a child just learning many academic concepts himself. Thus, she also asked Mrs. Ruiz to oversee Adriana's understanding of academic concepts when possible.

As Mrs. Wood walked around the classroom to monitor students' work, she noticed that Homero and Adriana were successfully completing the task at hand. She asked if they would be willing to share their solution with the rest of the class. Mrs. Wood told Adriana (through Homero's translation) that she would like her to share her ideas with the class in Spanish. She asked Homero to translate in English for classmates who were not fluent in Spanish. A few moments later, Mrs. Wood asked Homero and Adriana to show their solution at the overhead projector using a transparency and their plastic coins. Explaining their solution in Spanish and English, Adriana and Homero told their classmates that they would take Prize 2 (the prize that involved getting a penny the first day and doubling their number of pennies each day for the next four days). Using an overhead transparency chart and their plastic coins, Adriana and Homero showed the class how one would end up with $.31 this way and only $.25 by accepting Prize 1. Once they understood the concept of exponential growth, Mrs. Wood returned to the story and asked the children why Rani had been very wise. Together they summarized what had occurred and why Rani's decision had been so beneficial.

FINAL THOUGHTS

This sample lesson highlights the many instances of teacher-to-student and student-to-student scaffolding that occurred in Mrs. Wood's room. It also reveals the many opportunities among students, as well as between teachers and students, to engage in meaningful dialogue about content-specific information, to model English language use, and to advance the students' language and conceptual learning. Both scaffolding and facilitating constructive dialogue were important theoretical tenets that guided Mrs. Wood's instructional decisions.

Mrs. Wood employed a host of instructional features to support the learning of the English learners in the integrated mathematics/literacy lesson just presented. The overall framework she employed was the Prereading, During-Reading, and Postreading approach outlined by many educators, including Fitzgerald and Graves (2004). This framework is important because it emphasizes the importance of scaffolding instruction throughout the reading process. Recall that before the first whole-group lesson in English, Mrs. Wood asked Mrs. Ruiz, the bilingual instructional assistant, to read and discuss the focus story in Spanish with a small group of English learners. This activity helped the children to build background knowledge about the story content before they encountered the story in English. Mrs. Wood also reminded the children about the narrative story structure that they had studied in the past and asked them to think about how this story fit the story structure as they were listening to it. As the children listened to the story, Mrs. Wood directed their attention to the manner in which this story fit the narrative story structure. As she did this, she modeled how a reader should draw on evidence from the story to make assertions about the rising action, turning point, falling action, and resolution of the story. After the story, Mrs. Wood continued discussing the narrative story structure with the children and wrote the story events that made up the narrative structure of this story on the whiteboard, providing ample rationale from the story to support her assertions about the manner in which the story was structured. Additionally, she asked her children to address key questions about the story, modeling how to answer questions using evidence from the text in one's answer.

Mrs. Wood also taught mathematics concepts within the Pre-reading, During-Reading, and Postreading framework (Fitzgerald & Graves, 2004). Recall that she introduced the notion of exponential growth by asking her students whether they would prefer a flat sum of a quarter or a penny one day doubled every day for the next four days, if they won a contest. The children made their predictions in their journals. There was a great deal of Postreading activity as the class worked in dyads using coins and a calendar chart to decide which prize to select. Mrs. Wood helped the students relate this exponential growth problem back to the rice problem in the story.

Within this broader framework, Mrs. Wood also employed the following instructional supports for English learners (Wiest, 2008):

- Collaboration and communication. Mrs. Wood established a variety of participation structures (whole group, dyads, and small groups) whereby children spoke extensively with one another and the teacher to discuss the story and solve problems.
- Building students' background knowledge. Mrs. Wood knows that background knowledge (with respect to academic language and content knowledge) plays an important role in fostering children's learning. She did not just assume that all of her children had the same background knowledge. Rather, she was careful to assess children's background knowledge and help them build the background knowledge they needed to be successful in their lessons.
- Visual aids and hands-on materials. Mrs. Wood incorporated the use of visual aids throughout the sample lesson. The visual aids included diagrams and pictures. Mrs. Wood included the use of hands-on materials in her lessons as she provided the children with manipulatives to solve the initial exponential problem.
- Language support. Mrs. Wood asked the bilingual classroom assistant, Mrs. Ruiz, to provide instructional support for the English learners in both Spanish and

English. The ELs worked with study buddies who were fluent in both Spanish and English so that they could act as translators between the two languages. Additionally, Mrs. Wood encouraged the children to read and write in Spanish and English in her classroom. Finally, many important concepts and topics were written and labeled in both Spanish and English in Mrs. Wood's classroom. One of Mrs. Wood's goals was to demonstrate by her actions that she honored both Spanish and English in her classroom.

Regardless of age, all learners need appropriate instructional supports to experience success in the classroom and throughout life. In this chapter, we have focused on strategies for meaningfully integrating mathematics and literacy in a problem-solving lesson with special consideration for the needs of English learners. The instructional strategies suggested here will support sound mathematics/literacy concept acquisition and academic English development not only for English learners but also for the wide variety of students who populate today's schools.

CHAPTER 4

Thinking Like a Historian

Planning Integrated Social Studies/Literacy Lessons to Support English Learners in Fifth Grade

Kathryn Obenchain,
Julie Pennington,
and Rachel Salas

S OCIAL STUDIES TEACHERS IN THE elementary grades face the difficult challenge of teaching both "facts" and "concepts." This is not a simple task given that discussing and comprehending abstract concepts, such as heroes or crisis, often are sacrificed for the teaching of facts, such as memorizing the presidents in order of service. When facts are taught in isolation and disconnected from concepts, opportunities for meaningful learning are missed. What frequently results is that students memorize disconnected facts rather than learning them in a unified way as they are related to an abstract concept. Without this unified base of information as the foundation, teachers find abstract concepts difficult to teach, and students have difficulty understanding them. This is especially true for young students who are still concrete thinkers in their academic lives, as well as English learners (Brophy & Alleman, 2008).

We believe that both facts and related concepts can become an integrated instructional reality, as you will see by visiting Mrs. Weber's fifth-grade class. Fifth grade is often the time when elementary students first encounter historical content that is distant in experience from their own lives. Their previous experiences typically center around family, school, and communities that they can relate to directly. Mrs. Weber engages in a lesson-planning process to ensure that her students will gain an understanding of the abstract concepts of hero/heroine and crisis, while learning concrete facts about the Great Depression and the home front in World War II. The unit topic, "How Do Times of Crisis Create Heroes and Heroines?" includes lessons that support students' getting to know well-known heroes and heroines across U.S. history, with particular attention to the mid-20th century, while connecting to their own heroes and heroines. To facilitate the learning of content (facts plus concepts), students explore primary source documents as they work to understand the roles heroes and heroines play in times of crisis. In this way their language and comprehension are expanded. As Mrs. Weber plans and teaches her lesson, she also addresses the complexity of meeting the various needs of ELs and the reality that teaching is a recursive process that relies on continuous assessment and revision in response to student and curricular needs.

CONCEPTUAL FRAMEWORK FOR LESSON DESIGN

In her teaching, Mrs. Weber draws on her understanding of learning theory and the stages of English language proficiency, which provide a foundation for the larger conceptual goals of her lesson. As explained in Chapter 1, learning occurs within a social, cultural, and historical context (Vygotsky, 1978; Wertsch, 1998). Mrs. Weber values the experiences and primary languages of ELs and views them as knowledge contributors to the classroom learning community (Moya, 2002). At the same time, she is well aware that learning academic English is an instructional objective for students in the United States. She recognizes how challenging it is for ELs to learn new academic content knowledge and vocabulary taught in English while they also are learning English. She realizes that her students must learn both the general and specific academic language used in the content areas, and they must be able to use this language in class discussions and understand it in text (Bailey, 2007).

Figure 4.1 provides an example of the kind of detailed instructional plans Mrs. Weber creates that emphasize not only content knowledge, but also the kinds of academic English skills her students need to learn in order to successfully master conceptual

FIGURE 4.1. Framework for Fifth-Grade Integrated Social Studies/Literacy Lesson

Category	Conceptual Focus	
Academic language	Explaining historical significance	
	Reading expository text	
Social studies	Explaining how actions of heroes and heroines make a difference	
	Using primary sources	
Literacy	Reading expository text	
	Making connections to self, other text, and/or the world	
	Identifying the purpose of and gaining information from various sources	
	Writing paragraphs that include topic sentence, supporting details, and concluding statement	
	Instructional Approach	*Learning Theory Focus*
English learners	Use of visuals and realia	Scaffolding
	Discussions with teacher and peers	Scaffolding and effective social interactions
	Language objectives and language support (in Spanish and English)	Effective social interactions

content (Echevarria, Vogt, & Short, 2004; Heritage, Silva, & Pierce, 2007). While difficult for native English speakers in elementary school, learning conceptually based content is especially difficult for children who are English learners trying to understand complex concepts in a language that is new to them (August & Shanahan, 2006; Echevarria et al., 2004; Salinas, Fránquiz, & Guberman, 2006). The lesson we present in this chapter addresses two academic English skills related to social studies (explaining how actions of heroes and heroines make a difference, and using primary sources). It also features two primary instructional approaches Mrs. Weber uses to provide support to ELs, drawing and building on the background knowledge of ELs, and providing myriad contexts for collaborative discussions with peers as well as the teacher (Fitzgerald & Graves, 2004).

MRS. WEBER'S CLASSROOM AND THREE STUDENTS

Mrs. Weber is a White, monolingual English speaker, with 20 years of experience teaching elementary school; most of her experience has been in Grades 4 and 5. She currently is enrolled in a Ph.D. program in elementary education at a local research university, which draws a large international population.

Mrs. Weber is a full-time, fifth-grade teacher at Dogwood Elementary School, located in a mid-sized Midwestern community of approximately 200,000. Mrs. Weber's school has a very diverse student and teacher population, in large part because of its proximity to the university. Her classroom of 29 students has 16 ELs at various levels of English proficiency. For example, three of the students range from level one to level five of English language proficiency, according to Teachers of English to Speakers of Other Languages Standards (TESOL, 2006). These three ELs will be the focus of this chapter.

Carolina

Carolina, an 11-year-old native of Guatemala, speaks Spanish as her native language. Her family has been in the United States for six months. Both of Carolina's parents earned university degrees in Guatemala. Carolina's father works in a skilled position at the local

---

FIVE LEVELS OF LANGUAGE PROFICIENCY

The TESOL standards use five levels of language proficiency to describe the progression of acquiring a second language and attaining academic standards. They are, from level 1 to 5: starting up, beginning, expanding, developing, and bridging over. The World-Class Instructional Design and Assessment (WIDA, 2007), a multistate consortium (currently 19 states are involved), has six comparable levels of English language proficiency. From level 1 to 6, they are: entering, beginning, developing, expanding, bridging, and reaching. For more information on the TESOL standards and proficiency levels, go to http://www.tesol.org/s_tesol/seccss.asp?CID=1186&DID=5348; to access more information on WIDA, visit http://www.wida.us/standards/elp.aspx

---

auto manufacturing plant. Her mother works as a Spanish translator for a local social service agency. Carolina speaks English only at school and away from her family. Spanish is spoken at home. Mrs. Weber has identified Carolina as a level one student. Her English proficiency is emerging. Carolina is able to respond with words and phrases to queries regarding pictures and graphics. Mrs. Weber expects Carolina to respond to the hero/heroine concept introduced in the lesson, through understanding photos that depict people in need of help from a hero/heroine.

Elena

Elena is a native Spanish speaker and was born in the United States. Elena's mother emigrated from El Salvador 12 years ago. Along with her mother and two siblings, Elena moved from the western United States to the local community three years ago. Elena's mother is an academically fluent Spanish speaker and conversationally fluent English speaker. She co-manages a taqueria owned by Elena's extended family. Spanish is spoken at home. Mrs. Weber has classified Elena as a level three student. Her English proficiency is fluent at the conversational level and she is working toward acquiring academic English. She can use more elaborate sentences and some content-area vocabulary. Mrs. Weber expects Elena to access simple text and use conversations with her peers to gain new knowledge and content-specific vocabulary.

Javier

Javier, who is bilingual in English and Spanish, was born in the United States. Both of Javier's parents emigrated from Mexico 15 years ago and are native Spanish speakers. Both have advanced university degrees and are in academic/administrative positions at the local university. They are both highly proficient in academic English and academic Spanish. Both Spanish and English are spoken at home. According to Mrs. Weber's assessments and observations, Javier is at level five of English language proficiency. Learners at level five are able to use the technical language of particular content areas and complex sentence structures in their oral and written production of language (TESOL, 2006). Mrs. Weber anticipates that through reading and discussions Javier will understand the conceptual aspects of the social studies lesson as they relate to the roles of heroes and heroines.

THOUGHTS ON DESIGNING A LESSON ON HEROES AND HEROINES IN TIMES OF CRISIS

Mrs. Weber has a specific interest and expertise in curriculum integration. She believes that careful integration across the social science disciplines, as well as integration across other content disciplines, can lead to much more connected and authentic learning experiences. In particular, Mrs. Weber builds her curriculum and instruction using a curriculum integration model (Hinde, 2005). That is, she chooses meaningful concepts and questions that are

---

TABA'S CONCEPT DEVELOPMENT AND ATTAINMENT MODELS

While over 40 years old, Taba (1967) is the seminal citation for the Concept Development and Concept Attainment Models in elementary social studies education. Concepts are typically single words, like *democracy*, *movement*, *change*, and *map*, that describe a larger category of meaning. Concepts are typically very easy for students to find examples of; however, they are much more difficult to define because of their abstractness.

developmentally appropriate for her students, and then she looks to the academic standards in all areas to design her curriculum and instruction. For this unit of study, Mrs. Weber focuses on the social studies concepts of heroes/heroines and crisis. She is utilizing the era of the Great Depression and World War II as her social studies content. The students will need to learn many facts about the era and reflect on their own individual and collective experiences with heroes, heroines, and their own times of crisis to understand these concepts and their place in 1930s and 1940s U.S. history. The era and time period provide concrete and tangible examples to help students develop conceptual understanding of the social studies concepts of heroes and heroines and crisis (Taba, 1967). In addition, and essential to both history and literacy education, Mrs. Weber utilizes primary source documents (Hynd, 1999; National Center for History in the Schools, 1996).

Primary Sources to Promote Social Studies and Literacy Learning

Primary source documents are texts such as diaries, newspaper articles, photographs, legislative actions, letters, music recordings, and government records that were created during a particular period (Barton, 2005). Examples of primary source documents relevant to the lesson presented in this chapter could include newsreels, photographs by Dorothea Lange, presidential correspondence, and music by Woody Guthrie. Primary sources are the evidence historians use to build a narrative of an historical event or era. Historians carefully analyze this evidence to construct an understanding of a time in history. Analyses of primary source documents typically include three levels.

1. The item is subject to a *literal review or description* (e.g., what words or images do you see on the document? List everything you see in the photograph).
2. Following the literal review or description, the item is *interpreted* (e.g., What do you think the author wanted us to know? Whom do you think the intended audience was?).
3. Finally, the item is *examined critically and evaluated* (e.g., How important is this document? Why should we care about it?).

The ability to thoughtfully analyze primary sources is an important skill. However, a more important—and more conceptually rigorous skill—is the ability to synthesize multiple documents and evaluate the strength of each in order to construct an understanding of history. While an essential skill in history and social studies, thoughtful analysis of primary source documents is also consistent with literacy comprehension.

The trilevel method just outlined that historians use to analyze primary source documents is similar to the types of comprehension depicted by many literacy scholars. For example, Lapp, Flood, Brock, and Fisher (2007) describe four types of comprehension: *literal* (i.e., specific information mentioned in the text), *inferential* (i.e., what the reader can infer about the meaning from the words in the text), *creative* (i.e., what new/unique understandings the reader might construct as a result of reading the text), and *critical* (i.e., what ideas the text omits and why, who benefits/does not benefit from the ideas presented and why). Teachers can draw on the similarities and differences between these related, but different, disciplinary approaches to texts and their interpretation to foster their students' learning. One important difference, for example, is that primary source documents are not solely text-based but visual and graphic in nature as well. The visual and graphic nature of primary source documents can be helpful to foster the understanding of ELs because they can draw on different modes of communication (i.e., visual, auditory, graphic) to interpret texts (Brozo & Simpson, 2007). For example, the combined use of multiple primary sources such as photographs, artwork, and song lyrics, along with the more academic writing of secondary and tertiary sources (e.g., textbooks), allows ELs to utilize numerous modes of communication and background experiences in order to understand abstract concepts.

Connections to Academic English

The use of primary sources is also consistent with the effective instruction of academic English. Given that academic English focuses on language functions such as defining terms, explaining historical significance, reading expository text, and preparing research reports, students who use a variety of primary sources to construct their own historical understandings also are learning these aforementioned important aspects of academic English. In addition, academic English includes vocabulary that is used beyond social conversations. It is the vocabulary needed to communicate effectively in content-area classes and to comprehend texts in different content classes (Research Points, AERA, 2004). These ideas are mirrored in the TESOL standards as well in the conception of students at level five, or "bridging over" into the technical language of educational content areas. The academic English vocabulary associated with social studies typically consists of abstract concepts (e.g., *hero, crisis*) that are applicable across eras, events, and even content areas.

THE LESSON

The content standards in social studies that include distant time periods and experiences far from Mrs. Weber's students' lives are one of the main reasons that she integrates her curriculum around questions that cut across time and space. To begin the unit, "How Do Times of Crisis Create Heroes and Heroines?" Mrs. Weber helps her students to build a conceptual understanding of both heroes/ heroines and crisis utilizing a whole-group activity followed by small-group activities built on the concept acquisition and language skills of her students.

Whole-Class Read-Alouds with Discussion

Gathering her students in a semicircle, Mrs. Weber reads the picture book, *Sheila Rae, the Brave* (Henkes, 2003), periodically asking questions about Sheila Rae's experiences, knowing that her ELs can view the pictures in the story to help them understand the text. Sheila Rae has the reputation of being a very brave and competent little mouse. She is also known to be a little bossy to her friends, and particularly her younger sister. When Sheila Rae gets lost on the way home from school, Mrs. Weber asks students to share what emotions Sheila Rae might be feeling based on their inferences. Words such as *scared, confused*, and *nervous* are brought up. When Sheila Rae's sister finds her and helps her find her way home, Mrs. Weber asks the students to share some times when they have needed help and who helped them. While Carolina remains silent but attentive, Elena shares a story of being scared of a school bully and having her older brother stop the bully's behavior, stating, "My brother helped

---

MRS. WEBER'S USE OF SOCIOCULTURAL THEORY

Sociocultural theory underlies Mrs. Weber's instructional focus by providing an understanding of how social context plays a role in the co-construction of knowledge as she works with her students' background knowledge. The students recall their own personal experiences and have them validated as valuable sources of information in their learning.

---

me." Javier shares a story of getting lost in the grocery store and having a store security guard help him find his mom: "The guard was in a uniform and he called on the phone for my mom to come to the desk." These connections between the text and the students' personal experiences provide a bridge for the students' understanding of how they and others might experience personal crises and need a heroine such as Sheila Rae's little sister.

Once students have shared their personal stories, Mrs. Weber asks them to come up with some terms that could be used to describe what Sheila Rae might now call her little sister or what the students might call the person who helped them. As the students share terms such as "good person," "helpful," and "nice," Mrs. Weber lists these terms on the board. She probes the students to come up with a word that we might call a person who helps us during a personal crisis. Finally, one of the students says "hero." Mrs. Weber writes this word (along with heroine) in the center of the board and begins a concept web. Mrs. Weber understands that she is both building a conceptual understanding of what attributes a hero/heroine should have, and also bringing in vocabulary words that relate to social studies objectives. She asks students whether the previously mentioned terms (e.g., *nice*) are appropriate in describing a hero or heroine. Mrs. Weber draws a connecting line to the words *hero/heroine* for the terms that the students believe are consistent with hero or heroine. Mrs. Weber encourages students to continue to add words that are descriptive of heroes and heroines. New words, such as *strong, brave, courage, important*, and *Spider-Man*, are added.

The next day Mrs. Weber introduces and reads aloud *The Important Book* (Brown & Weisgard, 1990). Her goal is to work on the students' written language production using a particular text pattern as a mentor text, while asking students to use the vocabulary introduced the previous day. As she finishes the book, she returns to the text structure to highlight both the genre and the larger conceptual message in the book. *The Important Book* focuses on various objects, describing their attributes, with the opening sentence repeated at the end, which states the overall importance of the object: "The important thing about glass is that you can see through it." Mrs. Weber's goal is to model the writing pattern for the students, with the underlying skill being the analysis of the objects, which she will translate to hero/heroine attributes soon. To write about the most important aspects of a primary source document, the students need to be able to comprehend the literal meaning of the document and then describe the significance of the document in a critical way. Therefore, the end goal is to allow the students to work through the lesson and be able to create a text structured around the understanding of the importance of the hero/heroine. To promote the students' conceptual understanding, she has added another layer to her instructional design. Mrs. Weber understands the differing needs of Carolina, Elena, and Javier, and has assigned them to three different group activities and structures to deepen their understanding of the academic language related to the concept of hero/heroine.

Analysis of Primary and Secondary Sources: FDR as a Hero to the United States

The content goals of social studies at the fifth-grade level include learning about and understanding historical content. The United States in the 1930s and 1940s is so distant in time from the students; Mrs. Weber begins the study of this era with very concrete connections, building on what the students put on their hero web earlier. Mrs. Weber introduces the next activity by telling the students that they are now going to read some information and examine some documents that provide information about a time in history when many people in the United States were having personal crises similar to Sheila Rae's and were looking for a hero or good leader. To bridge the gap between the students' personal connections to the Sheila Rae story and their own class definition of a hero/heroine, she reinforces the parallel she has drawn between their personal crises and people who helped them, to people back in history who helped others, namely, President Franklin Roosevelt (FDR). While the crises experienced in the 1930s and 1940s in the United States were more than personal, involving national and international institutions, and including war, Mrs. Weber wants to develop the concepts of heroes and crisis by tying those concepts to the leadership of FDR during the Great Depression and World War II. She recognizes that heroes and leaders are not synonymous, but for the age of the students and the conceptual understanding she is developing, there are enough similarities to use the terms interchangeably.

Mrs. Weber asks the students to get into three groups she has preselected for this particular activity. The groups are populated heterogeneously; the students in each group are of varying levels of English proficiency and reading and writing abilities. To check for and further develop conceptual understanding of hero and heroine, and to provide a concrete historical example, Mrs. Weber distributes a different packet of information to each small group (full descriptions of the packet contents are contained in the sample lesson plan in Appendix C). Each of the three packets contains a variety of primary and secondary print and visual sources related to the topic, as well as a series of questions for each small group to address. The questions, which are successively more complex questions about the primary and secondary sources, were designed to further the students' conceptual understanding of heroes, heroines, and crises.

Group I—Biographies: Javier

The first group of students has a packet that contains a brief biography (i.e., secondary source) of President Franklin Roosevelt that one group member is asked to read aloud. Mrs. Weber has placed Javier in this group due to his ability to read expository content-area text and his familiarity with the concept of a president, which he had shared with her during the recent election. After the students listen to the reading of the biography, they discuss questions that address two things. First, they must recall their understanding of hero and how that is consistent or inconsistent with being a good leader. Second, they must determine whether what they have read about FDR qualifies him as a hero or good leader during the particular crises the United States faced during his presidency. This

> ## Understanding FDR as Human
>
> It is appropriate at this developmental level to include information that challenges FDR as a hero (e.g., Japanese American internment). However, this is just an introductory lesson. Subsequent lessons would include information about Executive Order 9066 and other information that problematizes the construction of FDR as a hero. It is important for heroes to be seen as human and fallible.

created the opportunity for the students to link their personal experiences with heroes and crises to the academic content under study. Although Javier's task in the group was not as the lead student reader, he was able to read along with the lead student reader and add to the oral discussion of the role of a president. Specifically, by talking about how his parents felt about the current president, Javier is able to articulate that the president is the nation's leader and that some people see his leadership as helpful. Mrs. Weber's placement of Javier in the group was successful because he could conceptualize the idea of a hero in relation to the role of the president helping people.

Group 2—Primary Sources (Photographs): Carolina

A second group's packet contains two black-and-white photographs of the era. Mrs. Weber placed Carolina in this group because she thought that Carolina—as a beginning English learner—would find it helpful use the visual sources in the packet to connect to the social studies concept of hero. The packet includes a photograph referred to as "Migrant Mother" taken by Dorothea Lange. This photograph shows a woman, chin in hand, with a child on each side of her, and an infant in her lap. For the photograph (primary source), the students are asked first to list the people, things, and activities in the photograph. Then they are to answer the following questions: (1) What emotions do you believe the people in the photograph are showing? (2) Do the people look like they need help from a leader? (3) Why do you think this photograph was taken? (4) What else would you like to know about the people in the photograph? These questions guide students through the three levels of analysis of a primary source document (i.e., literal, interpretive, and evaluative).

As the students examine the Migrant Mother photograph, they first note that the picture includes one woman and three children, and that only the woman has her face toward the camera. Next, they conclude that the woman's emotion is one of sadness because she is not smiling and her eyes look sad. They also say she looks tired, but decide that is not an emotion. They think she needs help because sad people need help. Finally, to answer the last question, they want to know what the children in the photograph look like, when and where the photograph was taken, and whether the person who took the photograph helped the people in the photograph. Carolina was able to participate in English in the discussion of the photograph because she understood the concept of a mother needing help. She pointed to the picture in response to the other students using the word "mother" and then added the words "help" and "hungry" when the students began to talk about the mother being sad. With the presence of the photograph and her beginning understanding of English, as she listened to the small group's conversation in English, Carolina was able to grasp the idea of someone needing help and that a leader could help.

Group 3—Primary Sources (Letters/Web sites): Elena

Finally, the third group's packet contains a letter written by a 12-year old Fidel Castro to President Franklin Roosevelt. Mrs. Weber asked Elena to be in this group because she felt that her developing English language skills would help her access the conversational English used by the young Castro in the letter. Practicing his written English, Castro congratulates FDR on his recent election victory and asks for $10.00. Recognizing the power in the office of the president, Castro reminds FDR of the numerous natural resources of Cuba, writing, "If you want iron to make your sheaps [sic] I will show to you the biggest minas [sic] of iron of the land." In addition to this primary source, students are directed to a Web site to read more current letters that children have written to American presidents. Combining the historical letter to FDR and Castro's belief of what the president can do (e.g., access money and make decisions regarding resources) with the more current letters to presidents, which also address qualities of a good leader (e.g., "A president must be honest and have integrity"), the students in this group must reflect on what they believe are the characteristics of heroes and leaders and determine whether presidents, both past and present, have these characteristics. In addition, they discuss how presidents display these characteristics. Elena was excited to read the letter from Castro because he also spoke two languages, and she was able to read the letters from children on the Web site that were about the important characteristics of presidents, past and present, with the other students in her group. These short and very simple letters written by children in English used vocabulary consistent with her current level of English learning. She tentatively used the word *hero* on her own during the discussion and added to her vocabulary words such as *honest*, *helpful*, and *strong* based on the discussion with her group members.

After completing the small-group work, one student from each group briefly shared, orally, the most important thing they learned from their packet of information. This was followed by a brief teacher-led discussion that linked the three packets. Mrs. Weber noticed that Javier, Carolina, and Elena were each able to share one thing they learned about the concepts of hero/heroine, leader, and crisis based on the sources their groups analyzed. Javier talked about how FDR was helpful even though he was in a wheelchair; Carolina shared how she saw a mother helping her children by holding them (she did this by pointing to the picture and saying "Mom helps"); and Elena talked about how Castro was brave to ask FDR for help and offer him something in return.

Individual Writing

As the final activity in the lesson, Mrs. Weber returns to her goal of wanting the students to be able to create a text structured around the understanding of the importance of hero/heroine in relation to perceived crises. She reviews the text structure of *The Important Book*, which includes a topic sentence/statement, supporting evidence, and a concluding statement. As her assessment, Mrs. Weber directs each student to individually write about either a crisis or a hero. Elena writes, "The important thing about a crisis is that it is scary. A crisis can make you sad. A crisis means you need help. The important thing about a crisis is that it is scary." Javier writes, "The important thing about a hero is that he helps people in trouble. A hero is a real person. A hero can be a president. The important thing about a hero is that he helps people." Carolina wrote "sad" and "help" for her assessment.

CONCLUSION

Mrs. Weber's knowledge of her students' various language proficiencies was helpful as she constructed meaningful and language-appropriate lessons for her students. She did not back away from using historical content and abstract concepts, necessary for quality social studies instruction. She recognized that primary sources provide all of her students a picture of the past, and some primary sources specifically further her ELs' understanding of complex historical content and abstract concepts. Her students complete the series of lessons within the overall unit understanding the concept of hero/heroine and crisis, and are able to discuss that concept in connection with the historical figure of American president Franklin Roosevelt and ways in which he (i.e., his administration) worked to help people.

CHAPTER 5

Designing Meaningful Integrated Instruction to Promote Academic English Proficiency

Some Tips for Teachers

DIANNA TOWNSEND, CYNTHIA BROCK,
DIANE LAPP, AND RACHEL SALAS

T HE TEACHING OF Ms. Miller, Mrs. Wood, and Mrs. Weber offers excellent examples of effective integrated instruction. Ms. Miller took us into her first-grade classroom and showed us how seamlessly literacy instruction can be embedded into a science lesson. Mrs. Wood showed us how literacy and math instruction can be a natural combination in a third-grade classroom.

And Mrs. Weber shared important insights about enhancing literacy while supporting students' interpretations of primary source documents in a fifth-grade social studies classroom. These teachers helped their students learn academic English as they taught literacy integrated with science, mathematics, and social studies content. They did this by expanding from the base of the children's home languages and scaffolding their academic language development.

Integrating academic language instruction into content-area lessons is certainly a challenge, especially when it seems like there is not enough time to accomplish even the bare minimum required in the school day. But we *must* view learning academic English as an essential element and embed language instruction into all of our lessons when so many English learners are being taught in our classrooms throughout the country. Like any new task, the first lesson likely will be the most difficult to plan. But once you start identifying the academic language possibilities of your lessons, it can become habitual and something of a fun puzzle. Think of it as cracking a code for your students, and then making that code explicit so that your students can continue to crack it on their own in other contexts. As shown in the classrooms of the teachers we presented, when students are able to transition between their home and academic languages, they become empowered learners.

GUIDING PRINCIPLES FOR STUDENT LEARNING

In addition to providing the examples in Chapters 2–4, which were designed as models to enable you to begin to integrate academic English as a dimension of content-based, literacy-supported lessons, we now highlight the three assumptions about learning initially introduced in Chapter 1.

- Student learning is enhanced when teachers strive to understand and base their instruction on the linguistic and cultural backgrounds that children bring to classroom contexts.
- Student learning occurs as a result of effective language-based social interactions in meaningful contexts.
- Student learning is enhanced when teachers (and others, such as peers) provide appropriate scaffolding to help students learn new concepts and language.

We revisit these assumptions in this chapter to enable you to see how they served as guiding principles to facilitate student learning in each of the lessons shared in Chapters 2–4.

In the following three sections we explain how Ms. Miller, Mrs. Wood, and Mrs. Weber used each of these guiding principles to help them integrate academic English instruction into the content-area lessons to meet the needs of their English learners. (Note that this kind of instruction supports *all* students, not just ELs.) You'll probably agree that these lessons are better content lessons because they incorporate language instruction. The chart included in each section summarizes how the three teachers used the guiding principles. There's also a section in the charts to help you think about and plan how to use these guiding principles in your own classroom. We hope you'll enjoy this built-in opportunity, while you're reading, to apply these ideas immediately to help with your future planning.

Guiding Principle 1: Student learning is enhanced when teachers strive to understand and base their instruction on the linguistic and cultural backgrounds that children bring to classroom contexts.

All students bring background knowledge and linguistic resources to the classroom, but what students bring to the classroom is not always the kind of knowledge and resources that are valued in, and sufficient for, school success (Schleppegrell, 2004). Teachers who draw on what their students bring to the classroom as a "way in" to content and language development are playing to their students' strengths. Two important things happen when teachers learn what their students can contribute from their backgrounds and also what extra scaffolding may be necessary to support continued growth. First, teachers help students honor their own backgrounds and resources; as Zwiers (2008) suggests, valuing students' individual ways of communicating is a way of valuing the students themselves. Second, teachers avoid assumptions that all students are well versed in what may seem like basic or commonplace forms of background knowledge or school-based communication. What may seem to English-speaking adults to be "basic" or "commonplace" in school language actually can be quite abstract, and all students do not have the same levels of exposure to it outside of school. Background knowledge is an important component of academic English because without background knowledge about a topic one does not have the needed information or academic language to discuss it or to comprehend what is being read (Hernandez, 2003). Teachers, like the ones we've introduced, use this guiding principle in very important ways in their practice to help their students develop academic language skills. As summarized in Figure 5.1, these three teachers showed that they valued students' existing linguistic and cultural backgrounds by planning instruction that enabled the students to develop content-area background

Figure 5.1. Guiding Principle 1, ELs, and Academic English

Guiding Principle 1: Student learning is enhanced when teachers strive to understand and base their instruction on the linguistic and cultural backgrounds that children bring to classroom contexts.

Classrooms	Supporting ELs	Building Academic English
Ms. Miller	Understood that not all students have experience with the norms of "academic conversations"	Provided explicit language to teach how to share ideas respectfully
Mrs. Wood	Scaffolded ELs with vocabulary and narrative instruction in Spanish and English prior to whole-class activities	Explicitly taught narrative structure throughout lesson
Mrs. Weber	Honored students' personal experiences of needing help in a time of difficulty or crisis; built upon those experiences to help students understand the concepts of *hero* and *crisis*	Used students' personal ideas about *hero* and *crisis* as a "way in" to analyzing the primary source documents, thereby allowing all students to actively interpret the documents

Now you try! Think of an upcoming lesson in any content area, and ask yourself the following questions:

How can you respond to your students' linguistic and cultural backgrounds?

What academic English component or background knowledge might you need to explicitly teach as a result of your students' backgrounds? (See Figure 5.3 for examples of linguistic components of academic English that you may want to address in your own lesson plans.)

knowledge, while also making academic English explicit. Let's review how this looked in operation.

Zooming into Ms. Miller's classroom, we saw that she recognized that students' primary or home discourses/languages were quite different from academic English, or the school discourse/language. Throughout the lesson, she embedded explicit academic English instruction into her content-area instruction. This made the "hidden curriculum" (Schleppegrell, 2004) visible to her students, which allowed them to be active participants in authentically "doing" science. For example, Ms. Miller did not assume that students had knowledge of how to listen to and share scientific observations. She explicitly modeled the language students could use in these conversations (i.e., "I have an idea that is different from yours." "Tell me why you think that."). Had Ms. Miller said only, "I would like you to take a few minutes to share your observations with your partner," her students' conversations might have been quite different. Their conversations likely would have been stilted and less substantive, and might not have included the academic tone and the follow-up statement ("Tell me why you think that") that asked students to provide evidence for their observations.

Mrs. Wood showed a similar respect for her students' backgrounds, by planning for *all* students to be active participants in her class. She knew that without the right scaffolding, it would be easy for ELs to default to lower-level thinking activities, as Iddings (2005) found to be the case in a second-grade classroom. Mrs. Wood's instruction guaranteed that the English learners in her classroom first were taught the vocabulary and narrative structure needed for later success, with resources in both Spanish and English, prior to the reading of the story. This scaffolding ensured that Adriana, Gabriela, and others could be active participants in the whole-class activity. In addition, Mrs. Wood supported the entire class in building an understanding of narrative structure. Rather than assume that all students implicitly knew the structure, she explicitly taught the components of a narrative and helped the students apply those components to *One Grain of Rice: A Mathematical Folktale* (Demi, 1997).

Finally, Mrs. Weber honored and built on her fifth-graders' outside experiences in order to support their understanding of the concepts of *hero* and *crisis*. After reading *Sheila Rae, the Brave* (Henkes, 2003), Mrs. Weber invited her students to share stories of their own experiences when they were scared and in need of help. She recognized that the abstract concepts of *hero* and *crisis* could be better understood, and thus transferred to other contexts, if students anchored their new understanding in already existing background knowledge. The use of students' experiences as the foundation allowed the students to understand *hero* and *crisis* in diverse historical contexts, including the Great Depression and World War II, thus allowing them access to and participation in academic discourse about these time periods.

Guiding Principle 2: Student learning occurs as a result of effective language-based social interactions in meaningful contexts.

To better understand this principle, let's start with a quick review of different kinds of language contexts. Bailey and Heritage (2008) have created a clear framework for the different kinds of language contexts students participate in during the school day. First, Bailey and Heritage distinguish social language from academic language; social language involves the informal, predominantly oral language of day-to-day interactions with friends, family, peers, and colleagues. Academic language is the language of schooling, and is divided into two categories: school navigational language and curriculum content language. School navigational language is largely oral language and involves communicating about general classroom activities ("form your work groups," "take notes on this topic"). Curriculum content language is both oral and written, and it includes content-specific language and text structures. Curriculum content language often is densely packed with meaning and includes many abstract and/or technical vocabulary terms. Students have different degrees of experience with the two categories of academic language. For example, ELs who have been in schools in North America for several years may be comfortable with school navigational language, but not with curriculum content language. For ELs relatively new to North American schools, both kinds of academic English likely will pose a problem. All students need clear modeling of this language and meaningful opportunities to practice using it in the appropriate contexts.

Each teacher in this book had some very specific, academic goals for her students. The second guiding principle tells us that, for students to build these abstract understandings, they need many language-based interactions in meaningful contexts in order to explore, test, and confirm and/or revise their understandings. How did each teacher provide her students with these interactions? Figure 5.2 provides an overview, and we'll now take a closer look.

To help her students understand a "big" idea in science, one that they could generalize to other situations beyond the instructional context of observing leaves, Ms. Miller had her students actually *do* science. Students had opportunities, in pairs and in the larger group, to make, explain, and justify observations. With Ms. Miller's guidance, the students determined a classification system for their

FIGURE 5.2. Guiding Principle 2, ELs, and Academic English

Guiding Principle 2: Student learning occurs as a result of effective language-based social interactions in meaningful contexts.

Classrooms	Supporting ELs	Building Academic English
Ms. Miller	Modeled explicit language and practice in large-group follow-up (e.g., "What do you observe about this group's classification?")	Facilitated students "doing" science with small- and large-group discussions around abstract ideas about living things
Mrs. Wood	Provided targeted language modeling and visual support to enable ELs' participation	Had students read, talk, and write about narrative structure and exponential growth in varying, and authentic, contexts
Mrs. Weber	Helped all students build concept knowledge about heroes and then created opportunities to collaboratively engage in historical analysis	Supported students' discussions of primary source documents with questions designed to promote historical interpretation

Now you try! Think of an upcoming lesson in any content area, and ask yourself the following questions:

What support will your ELs need to allow them to meaningfully participate in language-based social interactions?

What opportunities for meaningful language-based interaction can you provide to help students build understanding of abstract concepts?

leaf observations and engaged in scientific discussion about their differing observations. Ms. Miller's goal was to help students understand a scientific idea, *living things have observable characteristics*, and to practice skills of doing science (observing, classifying, scientific discussion). To reach this goal, she needed to provide opportunities for students to talk through ideas and engage in meaningful questioning. Had Ms. Miller's goal been for students to learn about the characteristics of leaves, a straightforward presentation of leaves with some built-in practice opportunities would have been sufficient. But she was focused on developing scientific language and thinking habits, and the activities with the leaves were simply the medium to bring students to a more sophisticated understanding. Ms. Miller's modeling of scientific-discussion prompts met the needs of all students for building academic language, but especially the needs of her ELs. Because ELs often have few opportunities to practice academic English outside of school settings, Ms. Miller's explicit language modeling was essential to enable *all* students to meaningfully participate.

Similarly, Mrs. Wood's goals for her students involved building understandings of a complex mathematical concept (exponential growth) and the components of narrative story structure. Starting with the first hook question about choosing prize money and the extra instruction for the ELs, *all* students had multiple opportunities to talk, read, and write using the language of both exponential growth and narrative story structure. In addition, these opportunities for the students to meaningfully use language came in different contexts, including the hook question that involved the students making a hypothetical choice for themselves and a story involving a young girl from India. Providing multiple opportunities to practice new concepts in varying contexts is a hallmark of good vocabulary instruction (Blachowicz & Fisher, 2000), and it is essential when building understandings of advanced academic content. To provide additional support to ELs in these varying contexts, Mrs. Wood provided extra language instruction prior to the lesson and numerous visual supports throughout the lesson.

Like Ms. Miller and Mrs. Wood, Mrs. Weber provided meaningful opportunities for language-based interactions to help her students understand complex social studies concepts. As described above, she wanted her students to explore the concepts of *hero* and *crisis* as they related to different historical contexts. In a large-group discussion, Mrs. Weber and her students explored the concept of *hero*, focusing on other words and concepts that are associated with heroes. The explicit nature of this discussion (e.g., "does *nice* go with *hero*?"), along with the accompanying concept web Mrs. Weber drew on the board, is particularly beneficial for ELs who are building new associations in English every day. After inviting all students to contemplate the language relating to the concept of *hero*, she gave students an opportunity to practice using that language with primary source documents. The practice of discussing the concept of *hero* with authentic Depression-era documents and photographs is clearly aligned with the second guiding principle, particularly because students' small-group discussions were guided by questions that Mrs. Weber wrote to promote authentic interpretations of the documents. Thus, much like Ms. Miller was teaching her children to "behave" like scientists, Mrs. Weber was teaching her fifth-graders to "behave" like historians. And, also like Ms. Miller, Mrs. Weber provided meaningful opportunities for students to use the language of historical analysis.

Guiding Principle 3: Student learning is enhanced when teachers (and others, such as peers) provide appropriate scaffolding to help students learn new concepts and language.

We are sure that providing appropriate instructional support, or scaffolding, is not a new concept for teachers, and you probably provide good scaffolding every day for your students. What *is* new is that recent literature has clearly articulated specific components of academic English to be included in the scaffolding process. With an understanding of these components, teachers can make them explicit for their students and scaffold their students' development of academic English. As a result, the "hidden curriculum" we mentioned earlier can pose far less of a problem for our ELs. We can help students crack the code of academic English, increasing their immediate access to content and their potential for long-term academic success. Let's turn now to those clearly articulated features of academic English, and we'll draw on Zwiers's (2008) work to help explain some of these features.

Zwiers (2008) tells us about bricks and mortar, drawing on Dutro and Moran's (2003 work, as cited in Zwiers, 2008) robust metaphor for academic language. The bricks are all those great content words that teachers identify as important content-area concepts for students to learn, like *photosynthesis*, *simile*, and *equation*. The mortar includes all the academic words and phrases that hold the bricks together. The mortar, arguably, is that hidden curriculum that our ELs need help with in order to successfully access content.

What are some examples of mortar here? Zwiers (2008) skillfully pulls from recent research to articulate those linguistic features that make up the mortar of academic English. Figure 5.3 highlights the features we'll look at.

FIGURE 5.3. Linguistic Features of Academic English and Challenges for ELs

Linguistic Feature	Description of Feature	Challenge for ELs
Figurative expressions	Metaphors, analogies, idioms, using concrete terms for abstract ideas, e.g., *boils down to, on the right track*	Students may not know the literal meanings of these phrases, let alone the figurative ones.
Explicitness for distant audiences	Assuming audience is new to topic and adding extra information to help them follow text	The majority of students' conversations may be informal, in which they don't have to elaborate on ideas.
Detachment from the message	The exclusion of emotion/opinions; the inclusion of logic and evidence	Students' communication may be primarily social, in which emotions and opinions are often present.
Evidence to support points	Using evidence to support claims and main ideas	Students generally do not have to provide evidence for key ideas in their social conversations.
Modal verbs used to convey nuances of meaning	Modal verbs express specific nuances in meaning, for example, *would, could, should, may, might, will.* "I *could* go to the library" vs. "I *should* go to the library"	Students may have difficulty sorting through all the possible meanings conveyed by modal verbs or may use them inappropriately.

Linguistic Feature	Description of Feature	Challenge for ELs
Qualifiers used to soften messages	Words and phrases that help authors soften messages and avoid claims of "absolute truth," for example, *seems, likely, often, generally, imply that, presumably*	ELs may interpret these inappropriately and form inaccurate understandings.
Prosody (stress and intonation) for emphasis	The stress and intonation of oral language	ELs' first languages might have different prosodic patterns.
Long sentences with condensed, complex messages	Long sentences often have multiple, connected phrases and clauses (including conditional, or "If . . . then . . ." statements)	Students may experience a "cognitive overload" in making meaning out of multiple clauses at once.
Passive voice	A common verb structure; the emphasis is on the action, not on the actor, e.g., "The data *were collected* in a laboratory"	Because not all languages have this grammatical construction, students might experience confusion over the actor and the action.
Nominalizations	Verbs that are turned into nouns or noun phrases, e.g., *creation, revolution, construction, execution*	These words condense meaning into sentences, thereby increasing the cognitive load.
General academic vocabulary words (Coxhead, 2000)	Abstract words used in academic settings across disciplines, e.g., *process, function, role, structure*	These words are abstract yet often not targeted for instruction in the content areas because they are not key content words.
Clarity	Efficient and effective language use	In both oral language and writing, trying to use all of the above components with clarity is a real challenge!

Source: Except where otherwise cited, descriptions of linguistic features in this chart adapted from Zwiers, 2008, pp. 27–39.

We'll look at some of these features in more detail as we revisit the classrooms of Ms. Miller, Mrs. Wood, and Mrs. Weber. However, in perusing Figure 5.3, you likely have surmised (notice our use of the qualifier *likely* here!) that the purpose of academic English is to convey abstract and technical messages efficiently. This means that students encounter abstract and complex vocabulary words, sentences packed with meaning via clauses and noun phrases, and nuanced language. Zwiers's (2008) work and the linguistics research on which it is based (from which Figure 5.3 was adapted) help us to better understand the specific features of academic English. We no longer have to lament the general, and often overwhelming, complexity of academic English and the overall problems it poses for our ELs; we can now look at our own language and the language of our instructional materials and determine exactly what language features might be stumbling blocks for student comprehension. And we'll do just that right now, starting with Ms. Miller's classroom.

Ms. Miller started with a key understanding that she wanted her students to build during her lesson. That understanding was: Living things have observable characteristics. What academic English demands are implicit just in this statement? Let's begin with the prosodic features, or the stress and intonation of the sentence. Most native English speakers would read this sentence with stress on the syllables that are in boldface here: **Liv**ing **things have** ob**serv**able charac**ter**istics. Imagine reading this sentence with the stress on the wrong syllables, like this: Liv**ing** things have obser**vable** charac**ter**istics. When prosody (the correct stress and intonation in language) goes out the window, comprehension is not far behind! Furthermore, prosody is always a challenge in learning a new language. Ms. Miller helps students, particularly her ELs, develop sensitivity to prosody by modeling language use and by giving students many opportunities to practice with the language. At the vocabulary level, the words *observable* and *characteristics* are multisyllabic words that are difficult to explain without using other abstract words; this is typical of academic vocabulary words (Coxhead, 2000). At the grammatical level, we can have another look at *observable* and *characteristics*. These words have roots and affixes. While Ms. Miller's first-grade class might not be old enough for extensive instruction with these roots and affixes, she certainly can bring students' attention to the idea that *observable* and *characteristics* have parts that sound just like other words they may know (i.e., *observe* and *character*).

Now, let's have another look at Mrs. Wood's lesson in Chapter 3. Along with her mathematics goals, Mrs. Wood had literacy and academic language goals, and Chapter 3 clearly illustrates the scaffolds Mrs. Wood provided to help her students meet these goals. In addition to her explicit math and language instructional goals, Mrs. Wood was implicitly building academic language proficiency in her students. To see how this worked, let's review the journal questions Mrs. Wood asked her students: Do you think Rani made a good decision in her request to the raja? Why or why not? Why do you think the amount of rice Rani received grew so fast in 30 days? Notice that Mrs. Wood uses words like *decision, request, amount,* and *received*. These are words typical of mature language users, also known as Tier 2 words within Beck, McKeown, and Kucan's (2002) framework. Additionally, these words are academic in nature because they have abstract meanings and have a greater frequency in academic texts than in conversational language. Mrs. Wood exposed her third-grade students to these words in a meaningful context. Furthermore, she was careful to read the questions aloud and explain them to her students before they addressed them independently in their journals. Here, Mrs. Wood met the needs of her ELs, in particular, because she did not assume they had sufficient familiarity with these words in English.

Let's look at one more aspect of these questions that Mrs. Wood addressed by reading them aloud and explaining them. There is a great deal of meaning densely packed into these questions. This is one of the hallmarks of academic English, one that is particularly challenging for ELs who need to unpack these dense sentences in order to comprehend them. In the third question, students needed to understand the phrase *amount of rice*, then understand that this amount was what Rani received, and then understand that the question was asking about the growth of that amount of rice. Mrs. Wood exposed her students to this dense question, but then scaffolded the students with her explanations to allow *all* students to access this academic discourse.

We now return to the lesson in Mrs. Weber's classroom in which her fifth-graders were learning to interpret primary source documents and to identify salient features of the concepts of *hero* and *crisis* from those documents. Following the small-group discussions in which students analyzed the documents, the students had to write brief descriptions about the concepts. For this writing activity,

Mrs. Weber provided very effective academic language scaffolding with *The Important Book*. Prior to examining the primary source documents, Mrs. Weber drew students' attention to the structure of passages in the book, which included a topic sentence/statement, supporting evidence, and a concluding statement. Therefore, before students even looked at the primary source documents, Mrs. Weber provided a model for how students should be thinking about presenting their conclusions. This helped to frame both the students' analyses *and* their writing for the concepts of *hero* and *crisis*. Furthermore, this model highlighted the importance of providing evidence for assertions, a hallmark of discourse in academic contexts. Without this model of presenting historical interpretations, Mrs. Weber's students might have engaged in less rigorous analysis and likely would have presented less coherent written summaries about their interpretations. For students who do not have as much exposure to models of academic English outside of the classroom, which is often the case with English learners, this explicit modeling of academic text structure and providing evidence for claims are essential components of effective integrated instruction. Figure 5.4 provides an overview of how Ms. Miller, Mrs. Wood, and Mrs. Weber provided scaffolding to help their students learn new concepts and language.

PUTTING IT ALL TOGETHER: INTEGRATING ACADEMIC LITERACY INSTRUCTION

Now that we've had a close look at how these guiding principles play out in the classroom, it's time to think about putting whole lessons together. We want to provide a scaffold for you, in the form of the following questions, as you attend to the academic English demands of integrated content/literacy lessons that support the learning of your ELs.

Step 1: Who are your students?

First, think about your students as individuals. Each one may share background characteristics with others, but each is a unique combination of traits and attitudes. The students profiled in this book may be similar to some of your ELs. Stereotypes just don't fit the bill here; our students are all multifaceted individuals. Keep in

FIGURE 5.4. Guiding Principle 3, ELs, and Academic English

Guiding Principle 3: Student learning is enhanced when teachers (and others, such as peers) provide appropriate scaffolding to help students learn new concepts and language.

Classrooms	Supporting ELs	Building Academic English
Ms. Miller	Emphasized prosodic patterns through her language modeling throughout lesson	Used academic vocabulary words in meaningful contexts to support students' understanding of them
Mrs. Wood	Did not assume familiarity with academic vocabulary words; provided explanations of the words	Exposed students to authentic academic questions, read them aloud, and explained them to help all students access the activity
Mrs. Weber	Provided multiple exposures in multiple contexts to *hero* and *crisis*, which served as multimodal "entry points" for ELs to build on their initial understanding of *hero* and *crisis*	Provided students with *explicit* models for academic text structure and providing evidence for assertions

Now you try! Think of an upcoming lesson in any content area, and ask yourself the following questions:

In a specific activity, what support can you provide your ELs to access the *language* of the activity?

What explicit instruction or scaffolding on a linguistic feature of academic English (see Figure 5.3) will you need to provide all students?

mind that no student wakes up in the morning wanting to fail, or to get in trouble, or to not learn. The kind of scaffolding you read about in Ms. Miller's, Mrs. Wood's, and Mrs. Weber's classes can empower students with academic language proficiency and make academic tasks more accessible; it can make a difference in their achievement and engagement.

Generally, if you have many students who do not speak English as a first language, heavy scaffolding with academic language should be a central goal in your lessons. Also, consider the number of students coming from homes at or near the poverty level. These students also need considerable academic language scaffolding, because they may not be receiving a great deal of academic English exposure outside of school.

Step 2: What are your instructional objectives?

Using the state standards that drive your curriculum (as the teachers in our sample lessons did), identify the instructional objectives that will be the focus for your lesson or lessons. Unpack the language of the objectives or standards. What academic language demands are inherent in those objectives? Take, for example, our closer look at Ms. Miller's objective: to develop the understanding that living things have observable characteristics. Here, we thought about the background knowledge students would need (living things vs. nonliving things), and abstract academic words (*observable, characteristics*). Also, Ms. Miller identified the key skills of "doing" science associated with this objective (observing, classifying, providing evidence), and provided students with meaningful opportunities to practice those skills.

Step 3: What academic English demands are implicit in the instructional tasks and assessments?

Once you've unpacked your objectives, start thinking about the sequence of instruction that will best support students in building their understanding of the language and content knowledge implicit in the objectives. In designing the sequence of instruction, think about opportunities for language-based, meaningful social interaction and the scaffolding for academic English features you may need to provide. Keep Figure 5.3 handy as you look through your materials, assignments, and assessments. What academic English demands are there, both content-specific and general academic? What do you need to do to give students explicit instruction and meaningful practice in academic English skills?

Step 4: Assessment—How will you know whether students have met your objectives and improved their academic English proficiency?

When steps one, two, and three are carefully addressed, issues of assessment can become less problematic. Once you know your students and your objectives and you've identified the academic English demands, assessments that will tap into student growth on the objectives are easier to determine. For example, consider Mrs. Weber's assessment, the writing task that students had to model after *The Important Book*. Mrs. Weber had the primary objective of building students' understanding of the concepts of *hero* and *crisis* in varying historical contexts, and she wanted students to show their understanding using academic text structure and with evidence to support their assertions. She also knew that she had many ELs in her class who might have not had explicit exposure to academic text structure outside of school. Thus, her instruction addressed both the concept knowledge and the academic presentation of ideas, and her assessment encompassed both of these as well. Had she taught *only* concept knowledge, and then assessed that concept knowledge within the format of academic text structure, her assessment might not have been valid. Similarly, had she taught *both* concept knowledge and academic text structure, but then assessed only concept knowledge, she would have gathered no data on students' growth in their use of academic text structure. The guiding principle for assessment, then, is to identify both the content-area objective and the academic language objective and to instruct *and* assess for both of these objectives.

FINAL COMMENTS

Those of us teaching in today's 21st-century classrooms face many challenges. Preparing students to be civic-minded, technologically advanced, and highly educated citizens is just the beginning. Add to this growing list of instructional demands the need to teach the academic English skills necessary to grasp basic and complex academic concepts to an increasingly culturally and linguistically diverse student population, and the challenges are compounded (National Center for Educational Statistics, 2000). We designed this book to address instruction in today's complex elementary classrooms.

The beginning chapter of the book established the social, cultural, and linguistic context of English learners in American schools. The middle chapters provided windows into complex public school classrooms with English-speaking teachers who serve children from a wide variety of academic, cultural, linguistic, and socioeconomic backgrounds. The instruction highlighted in these classroom stories focused on the meaningful integration of literacy and different content areas, with special emphasis on designing classroom instruction to foster high levels of academic English proficiency for English learners. This final chapter of the book provided explicit information on how you might go about designing the kinds of integrated instruction you read about in Chapters 2–4.

As we end this book, we invite you to return to the title of this text in your own planning and thinking about providing effective instruction in academic English for the English learners in your classroom. We know that the conversations we have had in the design and construction of this text have shaped significantly our own learning about providing meaningful and appropriate academic English instruction for English learners. We hope that the conversation we have engaged in here with you as a reader has positively shaped your own thinking and learning about this topic. We encourage you to extend the conversation with colleagues as you engage in the process of designing and implementing your own integrated instruction for the English learners you serve in your own classroom.

Integrated Science/Literacy Lesson Plan Using the 5E Instructional Model— Engage, Explore, Explain, Elaborate, Evaluate

LESSON TOPICS

- **Academic Language:** Negotiating meaning
- **English Language/Concept Objectives:** Convey clear and distinct perspectives and demonstrate solid reasoning
- **Science:** Observation, classification, and characteristics of organisms
- **Literacy:** Science talk

Science Standards K–4 Strand (*National Science Education Standards,* National Research Council, 1996):

- Life Science Content Standard:

    Characteristics of organisms
- Inquiry Standards:

    Employ simple equipment and tools to gather data and extend the senses

    Communicate investigations and explanations

    Use data to construct a reasonable explanation

Science Concept:

- Leaves from different plants have characteristics that are similar to or different from one another.

Science Process Skills:

- Observation
- Classification

Lesson Objectives:

- Students will observe different leaf characteristics and classify leaves according to their own multilevel binary schemes.
- Students will negotiate meaning using respectful language.
- ELs will negotiate and initiate science conversations by questioning, summarizing, and soliciting information.

Materials:

- String loops—five for each group of four students. Make loops by knotting together the ends of a one-meter length of string.
- Hand lenses—one per student
- Chart paper—one per group of four students

Science Trade Books:

- Simon, S. (2000). *Crocodiles & Alligators*. New York: HarperCollins.
- Patent, D. H. (2003). *Fabulous Fluttering Tropical Butterflies*. New York: Walker.
- Cassie, B. (1999). *National Audubon Society First Field Guide: Trees*. New York: Scholastic.

Advance Preparation:

- Preview all three science trade books and mark appropriate illustrations for the purpose of the respective lesson segments in which each will be used.
- Avoid illustrations that might introduce confusion or off-topic questions. For example, the crocodile book contains an illustration of a prehistoric crocodilian that should be avoided.
- In the crocodile book, find and mark the text segment that discusses the differences between alligators and crocodiles.

- Prepare large chart paper for each group with three boxes that model the binary classification system students will use.

5E INSTRUCTIONAL MODEL (BYBEE, 2002)

Engage

1. Instruct all students to sit together on the carpet in front of the teacher's chair.

2. Using the butterfly book, introduce students to the skill of observation. Ask students to observe and identify butterfly characteristics. Ensure that students move beyond the obvious characteristic of color or size to more obscure characteristics of wing shape and pattern.

3. Pose questions and bring closure to this segment using the Talking in Science Framework (Winokur & Worth, 2006).

4. Show students the front cover of the crocodile book and pose the inquiry question: If we were all at the zoo right now and were looking at a pond filled with crocodiles and alligators, how could we tell them apart?

5. Show 2 or 3 illustrations in the book and ask students to observe and identify characteristics they see. Specifically show the illustration comparing the snouts of an alligator and a crocodile with their mouths closed. The alligator's teeth barely show while the crocodile's teeth are clearly visible. Prompt students to name this as a differentiating characteristic.

6. Pose questions and bring closure to this segment using the Talking in Science Framework.

7. Introduce the skill of negotiating meaning using respectful language by asking students to come to a shared understanding of tree shape descriptions.

8. Point to the outline of a tree shape in the tree book and ask students to think about the best description. Call on students to share ideas.

9. Pair students and have them work together using respectful language to come up with a description they can agree on. Model appropriate language and actions.

   A: Shares description.

   B: "Tell me why you think that." Listens while A shares

ideas. Then says, "I have an idea that is different than yours." Then shares idea.

A: "Tell me why you think that." Listens while B shares ideas.

A & B: One may tell the other he/she likes the other person's idea better, or they may negotiate changes until they agree, or they may come up with a new description that both agree on.

10. Repeat Think–Pair–Share until you are sure all students are modeling respectful language while negotiating meaning.

Explore

1. Children return to sit at their tables.

2. Explain: We have learned how to observe and identify characteristics of living things by looking in science books, and now we are going to collect some actual living things—leaves—from the schoolyard. You will work together in your table groups of four students. Each person in your group will collect one leaf from five different plants or trees or grasses so that your group will have a total of 20 leaves.

3. After collecting leaves, students return to classroom and spread leaves out on their tables. Each table receives three string loops. Form each loop into a circle and place all leaves into one of the circles. Place the two empty circles side-by-side below the first circle.

4. Pose the inquiry question: What leaf characteristic can you use to classify your leaves into two groups?

5. Use group discussion to formulate a plan—use first steps of the Talking in Science Framework. Students are to observe characteristics, select one they agree on, and use it to place all the leaves with that characteristic in one of the empty string circles and the remaining leaves in the other empty circle.

6. Circulate the room to observe and assist students as they complete their task. Use questions to redirect when necessary and to check for understanding on an individual student basis. Students should understand that one circle holds leaves that have the *same* characteristic as the one they identified, while the second circle holds all the

remaining leaves that do not have that characteristic—they are *different*.

Explain

1. Ask groups to volunteer to share their classifications.
2. Use the Talking in Science Framework to pose questions and come to closure with each group.
3. As each group shares its work, write the group's selected characteristic in each of the boxes on the chart paper, and post the chart on a nearby wall.
4. Use the Talking in Science Framework to pose questions that bring closure to this segment. Be sure that students answer the inquiry question and understand the lesson concepts and skills.

Elaborate

1. Tell students that scientists often use tools to help them with observations. Distribute hand lenses to each student and model how they work. Allow students to explore the lenses using leaves in the string circle that do *not* have their group's selected characteristic. Leaves in the other circle that do have the characteristic should not be touched.
2. Ask students what characteristics they were able to observe using the lenses that they did not observe using only their eyes.
3. Post the inquiry question: What new characteristic can you use to classify the leaves from your old characteristic into two new groups?
4. Distribute two additional string loops to each group and have students place them side-by-side below the circle containing the leaves that show their previous characteristic. Circulate the room posing questions as necessary to redirect and to check for understanding. Students should understand that they now have a multilevel classification scheme and that one of the new circles will contain all leaves that exhibit the first characteristic they selected plus the new characteristic, while the other new circle will contain leaves that exhibit the first characteristic but *not* the new characteristic.

5. When the task is completed, have each group share using the same procedure as above. Draw the new boxes on the charts and write the new characteristics in the appropriate boxes for each group.

6. Use the Talking in Science Framework to pose questions that bring closure to the lesson. Be sure that students answer the inquiry question and understand the lesson concepts and skills.

7. Invite group members to select one leaf from each circle of their classification schemes to tape in place on their large charts to illustrate their characteristics.

8. For groups that desire a challenge, provide two additional string loops to complete the other side of the binary classification system.

Evaluate

1. Formative Assessment:
   a. Observation—observe students as they work on each task. Watch for behaviors and listen for statements that demonstrate understanding or lack of understanding of lesson concepts and skills.
   b. Pose questions—group and individual.
   c. Record evidence of individual understanding using a checklist of preselected behaviors that demonstrate understanding.
   d. Note the accuracy of leaf placement on each group's large chart.

2. Summative Assessment:
   a. This is the first lesson in the unit on characteristics of living things. This lesson has no summative assessment. At the end of the unit, a performance assessment will be administered that will include items related to the concepts or skills taught in this lesson.

Integrated Mathematics/Literacy Lesson

EXAMPLE LESSON

Grade 3 integrated mathematics/literacy lesson focusing on making academic English explicit for English learners and incorporating ESL teaching techniques

BOOK

Demi. (1997). *One Grain of Rice: A Mathematical Folktale*. New York: Scholastic.

LESSON OBJECTIVES

- **Academic Language:** Being explicit for distant audiences (i.e., writing clearly enough so that someone not present can understand a description of a situation as if she were there), supporting points with evidence, concept of doubling
- **Mathematics:** Problem solving and exponential growth
- **Literacy:** Narrative story structure

Prereading

1. If you have ELs in your classroom and a classroom assistant who speaks the language(s) of the ELs, try to secure a copy of the focus text in the target language(s) of the ELs. Ask the classroom assistant to read and discuss the story and key vocabulary with the ELs prior to beginning English lessons.

2. Ask students to imagine that they won a context whereby they could choose one of the following two prizes (display information on overhead or board):

    PRIZE 1 CHOICE: a quarter

    PRIZE 2 CHOICE: one penny on the first day of the week, two pennies on the second day, four on the third day, and so on, for a five-day week (number of pennies given each day doubles compared with the previous day)

    Ask which option students would choose and why?

    (Allow brief peer discussion time in pairs without figuring on paper. Note: Better choice is second, which results in $.31.)

    Tell students that they will return to this question after reading a story about a girl in India who faced a similar decision.

3. Tell students that they are going to hear a story about a very wise girl named Rani from the country of India who taught an important lesson to her leader (called a raja). Note: A raja is like a king. (Write the words *Rani*, *India*, and *raja* on the board.)

4. This story is a folktale. Ask students to identify different folktales they have already read in class. Ask students to share characteristics of folktales. *List on board*. Fill in characteristics that class may have forgotten. (Remind class about characteristics of folktales.)

5. The class will have already learned about the typical narrative story structure. Write this on the board. Begin filling in this story structure. Tell class that they will be filling in more of the story structure as they read the story.

    Draw a story structure outline on the board. This will include the following:

    -   Setting and characters (Do this before reading the story to give the students some background information about the story because it is set in a different country at a different time.)
    -   Rising action
    -   Turning point
    -   Falling action
    -   Resolution

During-Reading

Direct students to continue discussing the story structure outline as they read through the story, including the following:

- Rising action
- Turning point
- Falling action
- Resolution

Postreading

1. Questions: First ask students to answer each question with a partner. Then discuss as a whole group. If there are English learners in the class, pair each English learner with a student who speaks the student's native language and English. Encourage students to speak in native language and translate into English.

   A. Do you think Rani made a good decision in her request to the raja? Why or why not?

   B. [if not addressed with previous question] If you were Rani, what choice would you make and why?

   C. Why do you think the amount of rice Rani received grew so fast in 30 days?

2. Revisiting mathematics from earlier in the lesson: Keep the same partners/procedures as used for item 1 above. (First ask students to answer each question with a partner. Then discuss as a whole group. If there are English learners in the class, pair each English learner with a student who speaks the student's native language and English. Encourage students to speak in their native language and translate into English.)

3. Returning to the earlier question about the two contest choices of either a quarter or one penny the first day, two the second, etc., ask the students to tell whether the choice they made earlier is the same or whether their thinking has changed. (Explain.)

4. Using mental mathematics only, ask the students to try to figure how many pennies they think they would get on the fourth day if they made the second choice.

5. Ask them how much money they think they would get in total at the end of the five-day week for the second choice.

6. With a partner, ask the students to try to determine which of the two contest choices earns more money. (Provide play money or other manipulative materials to physically work through the problem.)

7. After solving the problem, students might be asked to write their final work on a transparency for easier sharing.

8. Ask a volunteer (or pair) to share their answer and how they solved the problem. Ask classmates to say whether they agree or disagree and why, and to ask questions of the student/pair who solved the problem if they have any.

9. Ask another student/pair to share a strategy they used that was different from the previous one. (Continue with one or two more if other pairs have strategies that were not yet shared.)

Integrated Fifth-Grade Social Studies/Literacy Lesson

EXAMPLE LESSON

Grade 5 integrated social studies/literacy lesson focusing on making academic English explicit for English learners and incorporating ESL teaching techniques

MATERIALS

Books:

Brown, M. W., and Weisgard, L. (1990). *The Important Book.* New York: Harper Collins.

Henkes, K. (2003). *Sheila Rae, the Brave.* New York: Scholastic.

Marzollo, J. (1994). *My First Book of Biographies: Great Men and Women Every Child Should Know.* New York: Scholastic.

Web Links:

http://www.archives.gov/publications/prologue/2004/spring/childrens-letters.html

http://www.loc.gov/rr/print/list/128_migm.html

http://pbskids.org/wayback/prez/buzz/index.html

LESSON OBJECTIVES

- **Academic Language:** Explaining historical significance; reading expository text

- **Social Studies:** Explaining how the actions of heroes and heroines make a difference; using primary sources
- **Literacy:** Reading expository text; making connections to self, other text, and/or the world; identifying the purpose of and gaining information from various sources; writing paragraphs that include topic sentence, supporting details, and concluding statement

WHOLE-CLASS READ-ALOUD WITH DISCUSSION

1. Read *Sheila Rae, the Brave* aloud, focusing on Sheila Rae's crisis (getting lost) and what we would call her sister who finds her (a heroine).
2. Build a concept web around the qualities and characteristics of a hero/heroine.
3. Read *The Important Book* aloud, reinforcing the text structure.

READING AND ANALYSIS OF PRIMARY AND SECONDARY SOURCES (EXPOSITORY TEXT)

Distribute a different packet to each of the three groups. Each packet has a list of directions glued to the front. Inside the packet are all of the necessary items for completion of the activity. This includes the primary and secondary sources and a sheet to record the synthesis of the discussion. Students will have 20 minutes to complete the activity. The first direction is the same for each group and includes the following:

Choose jobs for each person in your group.

a. One person in your group has the job of reading the chapter to the rest of the group.
b. One person in your group has the job of writing down your group's important information.
c. One person in your group has the job of sharing your group's information with the rest of the class.
d. One person in your group has the job of making sure that everything that was in the envelope at the beginning of the activity is put back in the envelope at the end of the activity.

PACKET 1—My First Book of Biographies

1. Use the Table of Contents to find the chapter about Eleanor and Franklin Roosevelt.
2. Read the chapter aloud to the entire group.
3. Find at least two things that Franklin Roosevelt did to help people.
4. Decide whether you believe that Franklin Roosevelt had the qualities and attributes of a hero or of a leader.
5. Decide whether you believe that Franklin Roosevelt was a good leader.

PACKET 2—Looking at a Historical Photograph

1. Examine the enclosed photograph of "Migrant Mother" by Dorothea Lange (http://www.loc.gov/rr/print/list/128_migm.html)
2. For the photograph:
   a. List the people, things, and activities in the photograph.
   b. What emotions do you believe the people in the photograph are showing? Do the people look like they need help from a leader?
   c. Why do you think this photograph was taken?
   d. What else would you like to know about the people in the photograph?

PACKET 3—Kids and Presidents

1. Read the enclosed letter (http://www.archives.gov/publications/prologue/2004/spring/childrens-letters.html).
   a. Who was the author of the letter and what do we know about the author from information in the letter?
   b. Who was the letter written to and what do we know about that person based on what is in the letter?
   c. When was the letter written?
   d. Why did the author write the letter?

     e.   Why do you think the letter was written?

     f.   What evidence is in the letter to support what you think?

     g.   What questions do you have about the letter?

2.   Each person in your group should write down answers to these questions:

     a.   What would you do if you were president?

     b.   What qualities make a good president?

3.   Go to http://pbskids.org/wayback/prez/buzz/index.html:

     a.   How are your answers to the questions similar to and different from what you read on the Web site?

After each group has had sufficient time to work through the packets (about 20 minutes), one member of each group shares with the entire class the most important thing they learned from their examination of the packet materials.

INDIVIDUAL WRITING

1.   Reinforce the text structure of *The Important Book*.

2.   Direct each student to utilize the structure to write about either hero/heroine or crisis.

Children's Literature Cited

Brown, M. W., & Weisgard, L. (1990). *The important book*. New York: HarperCollins.

Bunting, E. (2005). *Sunshine home*. New York: Clarion.

Carle, E. (1987). *The very hungry caterpillar*. New York: Philomel.

Cassie, B. (1999). *National Audubon Society first field guide: Trees*. New York: Scholastic.

Demi. (1997). *One grain of rice: A mathematical folktale*. New York: Scholastic.

Henkes, K. (2003). *Sheila Rae, the brave*. New York: Scholastic.

Marzollo, J. (1994). *My first book of biographies: Great men and women every child should know*. New York: Scholastic.

Patent, D. H. (2003). *Fabulous fluttering tropical butterflies*. New York: Walker.

Simon, S. (2000). *Crocodiles & alligators*. New York: HarperCollins.

References

Au, K. (2005). *Literacy instruction in multicultural settings.* Fort Worth, TX: Holt, Rinehart & Winston.

August, D., & Shanahan, T. (Eds.). (2006). *Developing literacy in second-language learners: Report of the national literacy panel on language-minority children and youth.* Mahwah, NJ: Erlbaum.

Bailey, A. L. (2007). Teaching and assessing students learning English in schools. In A. L. Bailey (Ed.), *The language demands of school: Putting academic English to the test* (pp. 1–26). New Haven, CT: Yale University Press.

Bailey, A. L., & Heritage, M. (2008). *Formative assessment for literacy: Building reading and academic language skills across the curriculum.* Thousand Oaks, CA: Corwin.

Barton, K. C. (2005). Primary sources in history: Breaking through the myths. *Phi Delta Kappan, 86,* 745–753.

Beck, I., McKeown, M., & Kucan, L. (2002). *Bringing words to life: Robust vocabulary instruction.* New York: Guilford.

Blachowicz, C. L. Z., & Fisher, P. (2000). Vocabulary instruction. In M. L. Kamil, P. B. Mosenthal, P. D. Pearson, & R. Barr (Eds.), *Handbook of reading research* (Vol. 3, pp. 503–523). Mahwah, NJ: Erlbaum.

Brisk, M. (2002). *Literacy and bilingualism.* Mahwah, NJ: Erlbaum.

Britton, J. (1983). Writing and the story world. In B. Kroll & G. Wells (Eds.), *Explorations in the development of writing* (pp. 256–278). New York: Wiley.

Brophy, J., & Alleman, J. (2008). Early elementary social studies. In L. S. Levstik & C. A. Tyson (Eds.), *Handbook of research in social studies education* (pp. 33–49). New York: Routledge.

Brown, M. W., & Weisgard, L. (1990). *The important book.* New York: HarperCollins.

Brozo, W., & Simpson, M. L. (2007). *Content literacy for today's adolescents: Honoring diversity and building competence* (2nd ed.). Upper Saddle River, NJ: Pearson/Prentice Hall.

Bruner, J. (1986). *Acts of meaning.* Boston: Harvard University Press.

Bruner, J. (1996). *The culture of education.* Boston: Harvard University Press.

Burns, A. (2003). Reading practices: From outside to inside the classroom. *TESOL Journal, 12*(3), 18–23.

Bybee, R. (2002). *Learning science and the science of learning.* Washington, DC: National Science Teachers Association.

Bybee, R., Taylor, J., Gardner, A., Van Scotter, P., Powell, J., Westbrook, A., et al. (2006). *The BSCS 5E instructional model: Origins, effectiveness, and application.* Colorado Springs: Biological Sciences Curriculum Study.

Calkins, L. M. (2000). *The art of teaching reading.* Boston: Allyn & Bacon.

Clay, M. (1991). *Becoming literate: The construction of inner control.* Portsmouth, NH: Heinemann.

Coxhead, A. (2000). A new academic word list. *TESOL Quarterly, 34,* 213–238.

Cummins, J. (1979). Cognitive/academic language proficiency, linguistic interdependence, the optimum age question and some other matters. *Working Papers on Bilingualism, 19,* 121–129.

Cummins, J. (2000). *Language, power, and pedagogy: Bilingual children in the crossfire.* Clevedon, England: Multilingual Matters. Available at http://www.multilingual-matters.com/

Cummins, J. (2001). *Language, power, and pedagogy: Bilingual children in the crossfire.* London: Multilingual Matters.

Cunningham, P. (2000). *Phonics they use: Words for reading and writing.* Boston: Pearson/Allyn & Bacon.

Díaz-Rico, L. T., & Weed, K. Z. (2002). *The crosscultural, language, and academic development handbook: A complete K–12 reference guide.* Boston: Allyn & Bacon.

Ebersbach, M., & Wilkening, F. (2007). Children's intuitive mathematics: The development of knowledge about nonlinear growth. *Child Development, 78*(1), 296–308.

Echevarria, J., Vogt, M. E., & Short, D. J. (2004). *Making content comprehensible for English learners: The STOP model* (2nd ed.). New York: Pearson Education.

Fitzgerald, J., & Graves, M. (2004). *Scaffolding reading experiences for English-language learners.* Norwood, MA: Christopher-Gordon.

Freeman, Y., & Freeman, D. (2003). Struggling English language learners: Keys for academic success. *TESOL Journal, 12*(3), 5–10.

Garcia, G. G., & Montavon, M. V. (2007). Making content-area instruction comprehensible for English language learners. In D. Lapp, J. Flood, & N. Farnan (Eds.), *Content area reading instruction* (3rd ed.). Mahwah, NJ: Erlbaum.

Garcia, G., & Wold, T. (2006). Hidden truths found in English learner data require some new thinking about academic language proficiency. *The California Reader, 39*(4), 24–33.

Gavelek, J., Raphael, T., Biondo, S., & Wang, D. (2000). Integrated literacy instruction. In M. L. Kamil, P. B. Mosenthal, P. D. Pearson, & R. Barr (Eds.), *Handbook of reading research* (Vol. 3, pp. 587–607). Mahwah, NJ: Erlbaum.

Gee, J. (1996). *Social linguistics and literacies: Ideology in discourses.* New York: Routledge Falmer.

Gee, J. (1999). *An introduction to discourse analysis: Theory and method.* New York: Routledge.

Gee, J. (2002). Discourse and sociocultural studies in reading. In M. Kamil (Ed.), *Methods of literacy research* (pp. 119–132). Mahwah, NJ: Erlbaum.

Giorgis, C., Johnson, N., Colbert, C., Conner, A., King, J., & Kulesza, D. (2000). Children's books: Characters. *The Reading Teacher, 53*(6), 518–527.

Gitlin, A., Buendia, E., Crossland, K., & Doumbia, D. (2003). The production of margin and center: Welcoming–unwelcoming of immigrant students. *American Educational Research Journal, 40,* 91–122.

Goldstein, T. (2004). *Teaching and learning in a multilingual school: Choices, risks, and dilemmas.* Mahwah, NJ: Erlbaum.

Harniss, M. K., Carnine, D. W., Silbert, J., & Dixon, R. C. (2002). Effective strategies for teaching mathematics. In E. J. Kame'enui, D. W. Carnine, R. C. Dixon, D. C. Simmons, & M. D. Coyne (Eds.), *Effective strategies that accommodate diverse learners* (2nd ed., pp. 121–148). Upper Saddle River, NJ: Pearson.

Heath, S. B. (1991). The sense of being literate: Historical and cross-cultural features. In R. Barr, M. L. Kamil, P. B. Mosenthal, & P. D. Pearson (Eds.), *Handbook of reading research* (Vol. 2, pp. 3–25). New York: Longman.

Heritage, M., Silva, N., & Pierce, M. (2007). Academic English: A view from the classroom. In A. L. Bailey (Ed.), *The language demands of school: Putting academic English to the test* (pp. 232–401). New Haven, CT: Yale University Press.

Hernandez, A. (2003). Making content accessible for second language learners. In G. G. Garcia (Ed.), *English learners: Reaching the highest level of English literacy* (pp. 125–149). Newark, DE: International Reading Association.

Hinde, E. R. (2005). Revisiting curriculum integration: A fresh look at an old idea. *Social Studies, 96*(3), 105–111.

Hynd, C. (1999). Teaching students to think critically using multiple texts in history. *Journal of Adolescent & Adult Literacy, 42*(6), 428–436.

Iddings, A. (2005). Linguistic access and participation: English language learners in an English-dominant community of practice. *Bilingual Research Journal, 29,* 165–183.

Kamil, M. L., & Bernhardt, E. B. (2004). The science of reading and the reading of science: Successes, failures, and promises in the search for prerequisite reading skills for science. In E. W. Saul (Ed.), *Crossing borders in literacy and science instruction: Perspectives on theory and practice* (pp. 123–139). Arlington, VA: National Science Teachers Association Press.

Kamil, M. L., Mosenthal, P. B., Pearson, P. D., & Barr, R. (Eds.). (2000). *Handbook of reading research* (Vol. 3). Mahwah, NJ: Erlbaum.

Krashen, S. (2004). *The power of reading: Insights from research* (2nd ed.). New York: Routledge.

Labov, W., & Waletzky, J. (1967). *Essays on the verbal and visual arts*. Seattle: University of Washington Press.

Lapp, D., Flood, J., Brock, C., & Fisher, D. (2007). *Teaching reading to every child* (4th ed.). Mahwah, NJ: Lawrence Erlbaum.

Lemke, J. L. (2004). The literacies of science. In E. W. Saul (Ed.), *Crossing borders in literacy and science instruction: Perspectives on theory and practice* (pp. 33–47). Arlington, VA: National Science Teachers Association Press.

Lenski, S. D., Ehlers-Zavala, F., Daniel, M. C., & Sun-Irminger, X. (2006). Assessing English-language learners in mainstream classrooms. *The Reading Teacher, 60*(1), 24–34.

Lewis, A., & Bachman, L. (2003). Measuring and supporting English language learning in schools. *CREEST Line*, pp. 4–9.

Malone, N., Baluja, K. F., Constanzo, J. M., & Davis, C. J. (2003). *The foreign-born population: 2000* (Census 2000 Brief C2KBR-34). Washington, DC: U.S. Census Bureau.

Moll, L. C. (1992). Bilingual classroom studies and community analysis. *Educational Researcher, 21*(2), 20–24.

Moll, L. C., & Gonzalez, N. (1994). Critical issues: Lessons from research with language-minority children. *Journal of Reading Behavior, 26*(4), 439–457.

Moschkovich, J. (2007). Bilingual mathematics learners: How views of language, bilingual learners, and mathematical communication affect instruction. In N. S. Nasir & P. Cobb (Eds.), *Improving access to mathematics: Diversity and equity in the classroom* (pp. 201–221). New York: Teachers College Press.

Moya, P. L. (2002). *Learning from experience: Minority identities, multicultural struggles*. Berkeley: University of California Press.

National Center for Educational Statistics. (2000). *Characteristics of schools, districts, teachers, principals, and school libraries in the United States— 2003–2004* (NCEAS Pub. 2006-313). Washington, DC: Author.

National Center for Educational Statistics. (2002). *Public school student, staff, and graduate counts by state: School year 2000–01* (NCEAS Pub. 2003-348-313). Washington, DC: Author.

National Center for History in the Schools. (1996). *National standards for history*. Los Angeles: Author.

National Council of Teachers of Mathematics. (2000). *Principles and standards for school mathematics*. Reston, VA: Author.

National Institute of Child Health and Human Development. (2000). *Teaching children to read: An evidence-based assessment of the scientific research literature on reading and its implications for reading instruction: Reports of the subgroups* (Report of the National Reading Panel, NIH Publication No. 00-4754). Washington, DC: U.S. Government Printing Office.

National Research Council. (1996). *National science education standards*. Washington, DC: National Academy Press.

National Research Council. (2000). *Inquiry and the national science education standards: A guide for teaching and learning*. Washington, DC: National Academy Press.

Nieto, S. (2004). Foreword. In T. Goldstein, *Teaching and learning in a multilingual school: Choices, risks, and dilemmas* (p. xiii). Mahwah, NJ: Erlbaum.

Piaget, J., & Inhelder, B. (1969). *The psychology of the child* (H. Weaver, Trans.). New York: Basic Books.

Research Points, AERA. (2004). English language learners: Boosting academic achievement. *Essential Information for Education Policy, 2*(1), 1–4.

Rockoff, J. (2004). The impact of individual teachers on student achievement: Evidence from panel data. *The American Economic Review, 94*(2), 247–252.

Sadker, M., & Sadker, D. (1995). *Failing at fairness: How our schools cheat girls*. New York: Touchstone.

Salinas, C., Fránquiz, M. E., & Guberman, S. (2006). Introducing historical thinking to second language learners: Exploring what students know and what they want to know. *The Social Studies, 97*(5), 203–207.

Saul, E. W. (2004). Introduction. In E. W. Saul (Ed.), *Crossing borders in literacy and science instruction: Perspectives on theory and practice* (pp. 1–9). Arlington, VA: National Science Teachers Association Press.

Scarcella, R. C. (2003). *Accelerating academic English: A focus on English language learners*. Berkeley: Regents of University of California Press.

Schleppegrell, M. J. (2004). *The language of schooling: A functional linguistics perspective*. Mahwah, NJ: Erlbaum.

Strickland, D. S., & Alvermann, D. E. (Eds.). (2004). *Bridging the literacy achievement gap, grades 4–12*. New York: Teachers College Press.

Taba, H. (1967). *Teacher's handbook for elementary social studies*. New York: Addison-Wesley.

Teachers of English to Speakers of Other Languages. (2006). *Standards and other initiatives*. Retrieved May 14, 2008, from http://www.tesol.org/s_tesol/seccss.asp?CID=86&DID=1556

Thomas, W. P., & Collier, V. P. (2001). *A national study of school effectiveness for language minority students' long-term academic achievement*. Report prepared with funding from the Center for Research on Education, Diversity, and Excellence (CREDE), U.S. Department of Education, Washington, DC.

Vygotsky, L. S. (1978). *Mind in society: The development of higher psychological processes*. Cambridge, MA: Harvard University Press.

Wertsch, J. (1998). *Mind as action*. New York: Oxford University Press.

Wiest, L. R. (2008). Problem-solving support for English language learners. *Teaching Children Mathematics, 14*(8), 479–484.

Winokur, J., & Worth, K. (2006). Talk in the science classroom: Looking at what students and teachers need to know and be able to do. In R. Douglas, M. P. Klentschy, K. Worth, & W. Binder (Eds.), *Linking science & literacy in the K–8 classroom* (pp. 43–58). Arlington, VA: National Science Teachers Association Press.

World-Class Instructional Design and Assessment Consortium. (2007). *English language proficiency standards*. Retrieved September 22, 2008, from http://www.wida.us/standards/elp.aspx

Zwiers, J. (2008). *Building academic language: Essential practices for content classrooms, grades 5–12*. San Francisco: Jossey-Bass.

Index

Academic competence, 6
Academic English proficiency, 12–17,
 22–23, 68–69, 77–94
  cognitive dimension, 15, 85–90, 91
  guiding principles for student
    learning, 78–90
  linguistic dimension, 14, 79–82,
    86–87
  sociocultural/psychological
    dimension, 16–17, 82–85
Academic language, 12, 55
  social language versus, 82
Adriana (student), 4, 5, 45–46
Alleman, J., 62
Alvermann, D. E., 2
Asad (student), 25, 28–29, 32
Assessment issues, 65, 92–93
Au, K., 8
August, D., 5, 18, 46, 64

Bachman, L., 2
Background knowledge, 47–48, 58
Bailey, A. L., 63, 82
Baluja, K. F., 2
Barr, R., 53
Barton, K. C., 67
Beck, I., 49, 89
Bernhardt, E. B., 26
Best practices for English learners,
  17–19
Bilingual education, 18–19
Bilingual support, 47–49, 58–59
Biographies, 72–73

Biondo, S., 46–47
Blachowicz, C. L. Z., 84
Black English Vernacular, 23, 26, 28–29
Brisk, M., 6
Brock, Cynthia, 1, 43, 68, 77
Brophy, J., 62
Brown, B. W., 70–75
Brown, M. W., 105
Brozo, W., 68
Bruner, J., 46, 53
Buendia, E., 5
Bunting, Eve, 1–3
Burns, A., 6
Bybee, R., 24, 30, 41, 97–100

Calkins, L. M., 28
Cantrell, Pamela, 21
Carnine, D. W., 52
Carolina (student), 4–5, 64–65, 69–70,
  73–74
Cassie, B., 30, 33, 96
Castro, Fidel, 74–75
Clay, M., 11
Code-switching, 25
Cognitive dimension, of academic
  English proficiency, 15, 85–90, 91
Colbert, C., 50
Collaborative conversations
  in mathematics/literacy instruction,
    55–56, 58
  in science/literacy instruction, 22–23
Collier, V. P., 2, 5, 15, 46
Complex conceptual processes, 11

About the Authors and Contributors

Cynthia Brock is a professor of literacy studies in the Department of Educational Specialties at the University of Nevada, Reno. A graduate of Michigan State University in 1997, Dr. Brock has focused on the areas of literacy and diversity throughout her career as a classroom teacher and currently as a teacher educator and researcher. Her research interests include studying how children from linguistically diverse backgrounds learn literacy in upper elementary classrooms and how pre- and inservice teachers approach literacy instruction in linguistically and culturally diverse settings. She also studies how teachers learn to engage in qualitative research. She is the author of books, articles, and book chapters that focus on literacy instruction in diverse settings, with a particular focus on how pre- and inservice teachers learn to teach children from nondominant backgrounds. Dr. Brock teaches undergraduate and graduate courses in upper elementary literacy instruction and graduate courses focused on qualitative research.

Diane Lapp, Ed.D., Distinguished Professor of Education in the Department of Teacher Education at San Diego State University (SDSU), has taught in elementary, middle, and currently high school as an 11th- and 12th-grade English teacher. Her major areas of research and instruction relate to issues of struggling readers and writers and their families who live in economically deprived urban settings. Dr. Lapp, who directs and teaches field-based preservice and graduate programs and courses, was co-editor of California's literacy journal *The California Reader* from 1999 to 2007. She also has authored, co-authored, and edited many articles, columns, texts, handbooks, and children's materials on reading and language arts issues. These include *Teaching Reading to Every Child*, a reading methods textbook in its fourth edition; a second methods text, *Content Area Reading and Learning* (3rd ed.); *Accommodating Language Differences Among English Language Learners: 75 Strategy Lessons* (2nd ed.); *The Handbook of Research in Teaching the English Language Arts* (2nd ed.); *Handbook of Research on Teaching Literacy Through the Communicative and Visual Arts* (Vols. 1 & 2); and *Handbook of Research on Literacy Instruction: Issues of Diversity, Policy, and Equity.* She also has chaired and co-chaired several IRA and NRC committees, and she is currently the chair of IRA's Early Literacy Committee. Her many educational awards include being named as Outstanding Teacher Educator and Faculty Member in the Department of Teacher Education at SDSU, Distinguished Research Lecturer from SDSU's Graduate Division of Research, and IRA's 1996 Outstanding Teacher Educator of the Year. Dr. Lapp is also a member of both the California and the International Reading Halls of Fame. She can be reached at lapp@mail.sdsu.edu.

Rachel Salas is a lecturer (currently on leave) and co-coordinator of the Urban Teacher Education Center (UTEC) at California State University, Sacramento. Dr. Salas has worked in the field of education for over 20 years, first as an elementary teacher in East Los Angeles and southeast Washington, DC, and next as a teacher educator and researcher at Texas A&M University, Corpus Christi, and the University of North Carolina, Greensboro. She earned her Ph.D. in education from the University of Texas at Austin. Her research focuses on the literacy needs of English language learners and the preparation of preservice teachers for an increasingly culturally and linguistically diverse classroom environment.

Dianna Townsend is an assistant professor of literacy studies in the Department of Educational Specialties at the University of Nevada, Reno. Dr. Townsend earned her doctoral degree in a joint program with the University of California, Irvine, and the University of California, Los Angeles. Her research focus is the literacy development of adolescent English learners, with specific attention to vocabulary development and academic English. Dr. Townsend's publications on her research on English learners and academic English include articles in *Topics in Language Disorders*, *Reading and Writing: An Interdisciplinary Journal*, and the *Journal of Adolescent and Adult Literacy*.

CONTRIBUTING AUTHORS

Pamela Cantrell spent more than 30 years teaching elementary and middle school math and science before obtaining a Ph.D. in curriculum and instruction with an emphasis in science education from the University of Wyoming. She is currently an associate professor of science education at Brigham Young University, where she collaborates with professors from various science fields to enhance in-service teachers' understanding of science inquiry. She previously directed the Raggio Research Center for Science, Technology, Engineering and Mathematics Education at the University of Nevada, Reno, where she was awarded numerous grants aimed at improving science and engineering education in schools. Her research interests focus on science teacher professional development, learning transfer, and science inquiry. She has published numerous articles in science and engineering education journals reporting on the success of her grant efforts.

Maria Grant is currently a professor in the Department of Secondary Education at California State University, Fullerton. She works with both preservice and veteran teachers in the credential and graduate programs. Her work includes research and publications in the area of literacy integration into content areas, with a central focus on science education. In addition to her efforts at the university, Dr. Grant's experience includes over 19 years of teaching in high school science classrooms. She has taught physics, oceanography, coordinated science, chemistry, and earth science. Additionally, she has acted as a leader in curriculum development and professional development at both the school and district levels. Her current efforts include professional development work centered on formative assessment. Dr. Grant received her doctorate from the University of San Diego/San Diego State Joint Doctoral Program.

Kathryn Obenchain is an associate professor in the Department of Educational Specialties (EDS) at the University of Nevada, Reno (UNR), specializing in K–12 social studies education. She earned her M.S. and Ph.D. in curriculum and instruction (social studies education focus) from Purdue University in West Lafayette, Indiana. She earned a B.A. in history from Hanover College in Hanover, Indiana. At UNR, Dr. Obenchain teaches undergraduate and graduate courses in social studies education, civic education, as well as general courses for EDS. Her research interests are civic (democratic) education and civic literacy, in both the United States and newly emerging democracies. In addition, she publishes in social studies teacher education with an emphasis in teaching history and civics. She is particularly interested in how classrooms are structured to promote democratic knowledge, skills, and dispositions.

Julie Pennington is an associate professor of literacy studies in the Department of Educational Specialties at the University of Nevada, Reno. A 2002 doctoral graduate from the University of Texas at Austin, she has focused on the areas of literacy and diversity throughout her 14-year career as a classroom teacher and currently as a teacher educator and researcher. Her research interests include pursuing questions related to how teachers approach literacy instruction in linguistically and culturally diverse settings. She is the author of *The Colonization of Literacy Education* and many articles and book chapters focused on issues related to literacy instruction in diverse settings, with particular attention to how race is constructed in schooling at all levels. Dr. Pennington teaches undergraduate and graduate courses in early literacy instruction and graduate courses focused on qualitative research methodologies.

Lynda Wiest is a professor of education at the University of Nevada, Reno, where she has been a faculty member since she attained her Ph.D. at Indiana University–Bloomington in 1996. Dr. Wiest's areas of scholarship include mathematics education, educational equity, and teacher education. Her national and international work in these areas includes more than 50 publications and several dozen presentations. Dr. Wiest is founder and director of the Northern Nevada Girls Math & Technology Program, which she has conducted since 1998. She serves on several national boards, including Women and Mathematics Education and the Joint Committee on Women in Mathematics. She was honored with a Nevada Women of Achievement Award in 2006.